THE LONDON
COMPANION

Jo Swinnerton

A THINK BOOK FOR

ROBSON BOOKS

It is difficult to speak adequately or justly of London. It is not a pleasant place; it is not agreeable, or cheerful, or easy, or exempt from reproach. It is only magnificent.

Henry James

THINK
A Think Book
for Robson Books

First published in Great Britain in 2004 by
Robson Books
The Chrysalis Building, Bramley Road, London W10 6SP

An imprint of **Chrysalis** Books Group plc

Edited by Jo Swinnerton
The Companion team: Vicky Bamforth, James Collins, Harry Glass,
Rhiannon Guy, Emma Jones, Matthew Stadlen, Lou Millward Tait
and Malcolm Tait

Think Publishing
The Pall Mall Deposit
124-128 Barlby Road, London W10 6BL
www.thinkpublishing.co.uk

ISBN 1-86105-799-7

Printed in Italy
The publishers and authors have made every effort to ensure the accuracy and
currency of the information in The London Companion. Similarly, every effort
has been made to contact copyright holders. We apologise for any
unintentional errors or omissions. The publisher and authors disclaim any
liability, loss, injury or damage incurred as a consequence, directly or
indirectly, of the use and application of the contents of this book.

London is a bad habit one hates to lose.

Anon

CAPITAL THANKS

This book would not have been possible without the painstaking research, cracking ideas, and dogged support of:

Dominic Bates, Paul Bates, Adam Biles, Sarah Bove, Anna Crane, Stuart Fance, Kim Gifford, Lucy Grewcock, Ivo Grigorov, Lisa Holm, Nikki Illes, Iain, Suzie, Anne and Niall Jenkins, Rachel Kurzfield, Charli Morgan, Jennifer Style, Nathalie Stahelin, and Iain, Angela, Alastair and Julie Swinnerton.

INTRODUCTION

There is always someone who needs to know when Big Ben first struck the hour, or who sold the first grapefruit in London, or what kind of fish swim past the Houses of Parliament. The same person would probably also like to know where in London they can find a spiral escalator, an audacious jumping spider and a tobacco pouch made from the skin of an albatross. If you know a person like this, you should give them this book, as it contains the answers to all these puzzles and many more.

But before you give it to them, have a browse yourself. Because then you will discover that Gandhi once lived in Bow, that the longest game of Monopoly lasted 70 days and that a vasectomy kit and a Chinese typewriter were once left behind on an Underground train. Once you know these things – and hundreds more – you will never look at London in quite the same way again.

Jo Swinnerton, Editor

LOST IN LONDON

The cleaning up of the Thames in the latter years of the 1900s has made the metropolitan waterway more appealing to certain fish and mammals who would normally keep their distance. There are currently 116 species of fish flourishing in the Thames, 30 of which migrate up and down regularly, within a few feet of the Houses of Parliament. Smelt are particularly fond of Wandsworth, where they spawn below the tide mark in March, whereas dace prefer to head for Teddington. So many flounder fry (young fish) migrate through Putney each year that they turn the water grey. Sea bass also swim through Putney, while grey mullet head for Chiswick.

The Thames also attracts more exotic visitors: a dolphin was spotted in the Thames on 25 June 2001, swimming as far as Wapping, Tower Bridge and Blackfriars Bridge, and another was seen swimming near Hammersmith in the autumn of 1999. On 13 June 2000, a porpoise gambolled in the river, to the amusement of crowds of tourists queuing on the South Bank to get on the London Eye.

HOW LONG'S THAT BEEN THERE?

Some prehistoric remains that have been dug up in London

Bears . . . . Woolwich
Buffalo . . . . St Martin-in-the-Fields
Crocodiles . . . . Islington
Elephants . . . . Trafalgar Square
Lions . . . . Charing Cross
Mammoth . . . . King's Cross
Sharks . . . . Brentford
Wolves . . . . Cheapside

DELIVERY NOT INCLUDED

In the 1920s a Scottish conman named Arthur Ferguson, posing as a civil servant, managed to 'sell' Nelson's Column to an American tourist for £6,000. He also sold Buckingham Palace and Big Ben before moving on to the US and parting with the White House and the Statue of Liberty. The buyers were unaware that they had been conned until they tried to collect their goods.

Ferguson was not the only one to try this trick. A man named Michael Corrigan sold the Tower of London, London Bridge and 145 Piccadilly to a number of American tourists, selling some of the buildings more than once. He also once persuaded the manager of a London jeweller's shop to lend him all the shop's stock for a day to help trap a gang of thieves, with predictable results.

LONDON WORDS

There was early coffee to be got about Covent-garden Market, and that was more company – warm company, too, which was better. Toast of a very substantial quality, was likewise procurable: though the towzled-headed man who made it, in an inner chamber within the coffee-room, hadn't got his coat on yet, and was so heavy with sleep that in every interval of toast and coffee he went off anew behind the partition into complicated crossroads of choke and snore, and lost his way directly. Into one of these establishments (among the earliest) near Bow-street, there came one morning, as I sat over my houseless cup, pondering where to go next, a man in a high and long snuff-coloured coat, and shoes, and, to the best of my belief, nothing else but a hat, who took out of his hat a large cold meat pudding; a meat pudding so large that it was a very tight fit, and brought the lining of the hat out with it. This mysterious man was known by his pudding, for on his entering, the man of sleep brought him a pint of hot tea, a small loaf, and a large knife and fork and plate. Left to himself in his box, he stood the pudding on the bare table, and, instead of cutting it, stabbed it, overhand, with the knife, like a mortal enemy: then took the knife out, wiped it on his sleeve, tore the pudding asunder with his fingers, and ate it all up. The remembrance of this man with the pudding remains with me as the remembrance of the most spectral person my houselessness encountered.

Charles Dickens, *The Uncommercial Traveller*

TOURIST ATTRACTIONS

London is the most-visited city in the UK, and boasts six of the country's top 10 tourist attractions:

Name	No of visitors in 2003
National Gallery	4,440,000
British Museum	4,800,938
British Airways London Eye	3,750,000
Tate Modern	3,895,746
Tower of London	2,019,210
Natural History Museum	2,729,924

QUOTE UNQUOTE

Her personality had an architectonic quality; I think of her when I see some of the great London railway termini, especially St. Pancras, with its soot and turrets, and she overshadowed her own daughters, whom she did not understand.
Angela Carter, novelist, describing her grandmother

WHOSE HOUSE IS THIS?

Where a few famous visitors found themselves a home in London

David Ben-Gurion (1886–1973), first Prime Minister of Israel, lived at 75 Warrington Crescent, Maida Vale, W9

Dr Edward Benes (1884–1948), President of Czechoslovakia, lived at 26 Gwendolen Avenue, Putney, SW15

Charles X (1757–1836), last Bourbon King of France, lived at 72 South Audley Street, W1 from 1805 to 1814

Mohammed Ali Jinnah (Quaid I Azam) (1876–1948), founder of Pakistan, stayed at 35 Russell Road, W14 in 1895

Napoleon III (1808–73), French Emperor, lived at 1C King Street, St James's, SW1 in 1848

Emile Zola (1840–1902), French novelist, lived at the Queen's Hotel, 122 Church Road, Upper Norwood, SE19 from 1898–1899

Jawaharlal Nehru (1889–1964), first Prime Minister of India, lived at 60 Elgin Crescent, W11 in 1910 and 1912

Lucien Pissarro (1863–1944), painter, printer, wood engraver, lived at 27 Stamford Brook Road, Chiswick, W6

Martin van Buren (1782–1862), eighth US President lived at 7 Stratford Place, W1

Vincent van Gogh (1853–1890), painter, lived at 87 Hackford Road, SW9 from 1873-74

Chaim Weizmann (1874–1952), first President of the state of Israel, lived at 67 Addison Road, W14

Mahatma Gandhi (1869–1948), philosopher and teacher, stayed at Kingsley Hall, Powis Road, E3 in 1931

Antonio Canal (Canaletto) (1697–1768), Venetian painter, lived at 41 Beak Street, W1

Washington Irving (1783–1859), American writer, lived at 8 Argyll Street, W1

Prince Talleyrand (1754–1838), French statesman and diplomat lived at 21 Hanover Square, W1

QUOTE UNQUOTE

London doesn't love the latent or the lurking, has neither time, nor taste, nor sense for anything less discernible than the red flag in front of the steam-roller. It wants cash over the counter and letters ten feet high.
Henry James, US novelist

LONDON FROM A BUS

The Number 11 bus is London's unofficial sightseeing bus. Its normal route takes it past the Bank of England, St Mary le Bow, St Paul's (look across the river for a view along the Millennium Bridge to the Tate Modern), Fleet Street, the Royal Courts of Justice, the Aldwych, and Somerset House. It then motors along the Strand to Charing Cross, Trafalgar Square, Whitehall (Downing Street, Horse Guards Parade), to Westminster for the Houses of Parliament and the Clock Tower, past Westminster Abbey and Westminster Cathedral, offers a view across St James's Park to Buckingham Palace, calls in at Victoria Station, then heads for Sloane Square and the King's Road, before coming to a halt at Fulham Broadway.

The Number 11 enjoyed a brief moment of notoriety on Jubilee Day in 2002 when 40 police officers arrested 19 anti-monarchist protesters in a pub, allegedly for breach of the peace. Short of a police vehicle large enough to hold them all, the police flagged down a Number 11, bundled the men and four other protesters on to the bus, then drove around London for two and a half hours, dropping them off at police stations around the capital. Scotland Yard praised its officers' ingenuity, but the courts disagreed. The aggrieved protesters – none of whom was eventually charged – took the Met to court, and received a settlement of £80,000 and an apology.

CAPITAL CONUNDRUMS

Where is the centre of London?
Answer on page 153.

SIGNIFICANT STATUES

Nelson's Column

When Admiral Nelson was mortally wounded by a musket ball at the Battle of Trafalgar in 1805, he might have been gratified to know that a statue of him would remain for ever at the heart of London, in a square named after his last battle. In Trafalgar Square stands Nelson's Column, which measures 185 feet high, including the 18-foot statue of Nelson. The bronze relief sculptures around the base are made out of captured French cannons and depict the Admiral's victories at Copenhagen, the Nile and Cape St Vincent as well as Trafalgar. Nelson's remains are buried in St Paul's Cathedral, and his monument includes a stirring call to prayer that he wrote before the Battle of Trafalgar, as the enemy approached. Some say that the reason he faces south is to watch over his fleet of ships on top of the Mall lampposts.

On the first visit to his new Mayfair club, Bertie was delighted to find there was almost nothing that he wasn't allowed to do

LONDON LEGENDS

George Peabody

The name Peabody is familiar on both sides of the Atlantic thanks to a generous American whose substantial fortune has provided housing for unfortunate Londoners for hundreds of years. George Peabody was a successful merchant and banker in the US before he moved to London to continue his profession, where he soon amassed a fortune. Part of it was spent creating art galleries, libraries and museums in the US, but he was so appalled by the slums of London that he also gave $2.5 million to fund the building of blocks of flats for the impoverished, which continue today as the Peabody Trust. He was the first American to be given the freedom of the city, and a vast crowd attended his funeral in London. His Trust still provides 19,500 homes, there are 30 references to his name in the index of the A–Z and he is commemorated by a statue in Threadneedle Street.

14 *Amount, to the closest inch, that 1 Canada Square is designed to sway in the strongest wind (13.75" to be precise)*

London is alleged to be awash with ghosts, all haunting the scenes of their demise. Here are a few of the many lost souls:

Bank
Haunted by the Bank Nun, whose brother was executed 200 years ago for dealing in forged bank notes. His grieving sister now waits for ever for his return.

Bank Station
When this station was built, the work disturbed a graveyard, and staff have reported feelings of dread and strange smells – like that of a newly opened grave.

British Museum
Haunted by a Priestess of the Temple of Amen-Ra. The evil spirits are said to emanate from a coffin lid in the Egyptian Room.

Covent Garden Station
Haunted by William Terriss, who was murdered in Maiden Lane in 1897. The staff are often excused from working there at night.

Farringdon Station
Haunted by the screams of Anne Naylor, aged 13, who was murdered in 1798 in a milliner's shop near to the station's site.

Hampton Court
Hit the headlines in 2003 when CCTV footage captured the movements of a ghostly figure.

North Kensington
Haunted by a driverless ghostly bus so lifelike that it has forced motorists off the road. Has not been seen since alterations to a junction on St Mark's Road made the road safer.

Old Bailey
This stands on the site of Newgate prison and is said to be haunted by a prisoner in the form of a snarling hound, who was killed and eaten by his fellow prisoners, crazed with starvation.

St James's Palace
Haunted by a Mr Sellis, the valet of the Duke of Cumberland. Sellis's daughter killed herself after she was impregnated by the Duke. Sellis's throat was cut, perhaps to stop him from spilling the beans or from taking revenge.

St Thomas's Hospital
Haunted by a middle-aged lady in a grey uniform, who appears to those who are about to die. She is seen only from mid-calf upwards, thought to be because the floors were raised when the hospital was rebuilt.

Theatre Royal, Drury Lane
The pale figure of a man with a tricorn hat has been seen in the fourth row of the upper circle. A sighting of him during rehearsals is supposed to bode well for the success of the show.

Westminster Abbey
The ghost of a soldier has been seen standing over the Tomb of the Unknown Soldier, guarding its fallen comrade.

SPORTING LONDON

The London Olympics in 1908 proved to be the country's most successful in Olympic history. That year, UK athletes won a total of 142 medals: 56 gold, 51 silver and 35 bronze. They stand fourth in the league table of most successful countries at a single Olympic competition, surpassed only by the USA in 1904 and 1984, and the USSR in 1980, who won 242, 174 and 195 medals respectively.

POPULATION STATISTICS

London statistics from the 2001 census

- Number of male residents: 3,468,793
- Number of female residents: 3,703,298
- Number of residents aged 15 and under: 1,448,236
- Number of residents aged 15–74: 5,300,332
- Number of residents aged 75 and over: 423,523
- The most populated age band is 30–34: there were 696,005 residents in this age band
- The most populated age band for men was 30–34 (341,087); for women it was 25–29 (360,393)
- There were 37,267 people aged 90 and over living in London
- There were 2,359,932 single people living in London (who have never been married)
- There were 2,386,210 married or remarried people living in London
- There were 1,046,888 people living alone in London
- 31,960 households didn't have their own bath, shower or toilet
- 522,471 households were living in overcrowded premises
- 5,229,187 of London's residents were born in the UK
- The largest religious group was Christian (4,176,175)

IT'S RENT DAY AGAIN

Every year, a strange and very ancient ceremony is enacted at the High Court on the Strand. Called the Horseshoe and Faggott Cutting Ceremony, it recreates the payment due for rent on two pieces of land. For the first, the City Solicitor presents two hazel rods to the Queen's Remembrancer, who replies 'Good service,' which settles the rent on the Moors at Eardington in Shropshire. Then a second payment is made in the form of six horseshoes and 61 nails, to which the Remembrancer replies 'Good number.' This is the rent for the piece of land on which Australia House now stands. It is not a public ceremony, though one can apply to watch; and no one is entirely sure if the rent paid is the right amount, as it was all rather a long time ago.

WHEN TERMINAL MEANS TERMINAL

The London Necropolis Railway was a dedicated train line that once carried the deceased to their final resting-place at Brookwood Cemetery. When the cemetery and railway opened in 1854, there were objections to dead bodies being transported in such an undignified manner, but it was thought the only practical way for the coffins to make the 25-mile journey from London. The trains began their journey at the London Necropolis Station, the entrance to which still exists at 121 Westminster Bridge Road. When the trains neared Brookwood's mainline station, they had to reverse discreetly into the cemetery termini: South Station for the Anglican coffins and North Station for the nonconformists. Mourners could accompany the bodies on the train to the cemetery, although the train company, somewhat insensitively, sold one-way tickets only. The Necropolis Railway operated until its Waterloo terminal was bombed in 1941, after which the service was never resumed.

BRIDGE OVER TROUBLED WATERS

Blackfriars Bridge has a long history, but is perhaps most famous for being the execution site of Roberto Calvi, found hanging under the bridge on 18 June 1982, with his pockets full of bricks. No one was convicted of his murder, but it was widely rumoured that the Sicilian Mafia were taking their revenge on the unfortunate banker, as he had lost some money that he borrowed from them to bail out the bank of which he was chairman. The Mafia got their money back – but it was too late for Calvi.

LONDON WORDS

On the north side of Lincoln's Inn Fields, beyond the handsome Inns of Court Hotel, is the eccentric Soane Museum, formed in his own house and bequeathed to the nation by Sir John Soane, who was the son of a bricklayer at Reading, but, being distinguished as a student in the Royal Academy, and sent to Rome with the Academy pension, lived to become the architect of the Bank of England. The museum, which Mrs Jameson calls 'a fairy palace of virtu', was especially intended by its founder to illustrate the artistic and instructive purposes to which it is possible to devote an English private residence... Few people know of it, and fewer visit it, which is much to be regretted, since, though, as Dr Waagen says, the overcrowded and labyrinthine house leaves an impression as of a feverish dream, it contains, together with much rubbish, several most interesting pictures.

Augustus Hare, *Walks in London*

Pearly Kings and Queens

The Pearly Kings and Queens are one of London's best-known eccentric traditions, although they are still a mystery to many of the city's residents. The tradition began in the late nineteenth century with Henry Croft, an orphan, who walked the streets collecting money for charity in between his road-sweeping job. It was the custom for many street traders to sew a few pearl buttons on his suit, so to attract attention, Croft covered his clothes in buttons, and found that his takings increased. He recruited a few friends to do the same, and the charity was born.

The first real Pearly society was formed in 1911, in Finchley, and became a close-knit community. When Croft died in 1930, 400 Pearlies turned out to mourn him and the event was covered by Pathe News. Since then the Pearlies have developed their own dynasty, comprising many kings and queens, each ruling over their own patch, from Clapton to Westminster. Unfortunately, like the real Royal Family, feuds and fallings-out are commonplace. In the Original London Pearly Kings and Queens Association, the word 'original' speaks volumes. In 2001, Pat Jolly, the Pearly King of Crystal Palace, defended the Pearly Queen of Harrow against charges of mishandling the books and was thrown out of the organisation for his pains. So he set up a breakaway movement called the London Pearly Kings and Queens Society. There is also another group of breakaways, the Pearly Guild. The Association is based at St Martin's, the Society at St Paul's and the Guild at St Mary-le-Bow, and despite their differences, all three work tirelessly through the year, raising money for London charities.

CLASSICAL LONDON WORKS

'Cockaigne (in London Town)', *Edward Elgar*
'In Honour of the City of London', *William Walton*
'A London Overture', *John Ireland*
'A London Symphony', *Ralph Vaughan Williams*

A TRIP DOWN CAREY STREET

'To be in Carey Street' was a popular euphemism for being in financial trouble. Carey Street, a small street behind the Royal Courts of Justice, has been home to the Bankruptcy Court since 1840, so there was a good chance that anyone walking down it was already in the red. The Seven Stars Pub, which opened in 1602, is one of very few buildings in central London to have survived the fire of 1666 and is still serving a consoling pint to anyone down on their luck.

Amount, in pounds, that the average London resident spent on public transport each week in 2000

*On hearing that London was bidding for the next Olympics,
Lucy stepped up her training regime*

WATCH OUT, BEADLES ABOUT

To ensure that proper behaviour was observed in his upmarket shopping mall, Burlington Arcade, Lord George Cavendish created his own corps of bouncers, known as the Burlington Arcade Beadles, all of whom were recruited from his own regiment of the 10th Hussars. The Beadles' job when the arcade opened in 1819 was to uphold decorum under its elegant arches, which meant no singing, humming, running, dancing or opening umbrellas – rules they continue to enforce to this day, while dressed in the original uniform of Edwardian frock coats and gold-braided top hats.

The most expensive painting in the world was sold in London, by Sotheby's on 10 July 2002. *Massacre of the Innocents* by Peter Paul Rubens went for £45 million.

Sotheby's also handled the sale of the most expensive piece of sculpture sold in the UK, Edgar Degas' *Petite Danseuse de Quatorze Ans*, which sold for £7 million on 27 June 2000.

Christie's in London holds the distinction of selling the most expensive gouache or pastel work in the world, Picasso's *Acrobate et Jeune Arlequin*, which sold for £19 million on 28 November 1988.

The most expensive musical instrument was sold in an online auction in the Hard Rock Cafés in London and New York on 17 October 2000. John Lennon's Steinway Model Z piano, complete with cigarette burns, which Lennon played at Woodstock, went for £1,450,000.

The next most expensive instrument was Stradivari's Kreutzer violin, sold by Christie's in London on 1 April 1998 for £946,000.

LONDON WORDS

A fine October morning in the north east suburbs of London, a vast district many miles away from the London of Mayfair and St. James's, much less known there than the Paris of the Rue de Rivoli and the Champs Elysees, and much less narrow, squalid, fetid and airless in its slums; strong in comfortable, prosperous middle class life; wide-streeted, myriad-populated; well-served with ugly iron urinals, Radical clubs, tram lines, and a perpetual stream of yellow cars; enjoying in its main thoroughfares the luxury of grass-grown 'front gardens,' untrodden by the foot of man save as to the path from the gate to the hall door; but blighted by an intolerable monotony of miles and miles of graceless, characterless brick houses, black iron railings, stony pavements, slaty roofs, and respectably ill dressed or disreputably poorly dressed people, quite accustomed to the place, and mostly plodding about somebody else's work, which they would not do if they themselves could help it. The little energy and eagerness that crop up show themselves in cockney cupidity and business 'push.' Even the policemen and the chapels are not infrequent enough to break the monotony. The sun is shining cheerfully; there is no fog; and though the smoke effectually prevents anything, whether faces and hands or bricks and mortar, from looking fresh and clean, it is not hanging heavily enough to trouble a Londoner.

George Bernard Shaw, *Candida:* opening stage directions for Act I

COCKNEY

The word 'Cockney' has been used freely, though not always politely, to describe a certain kind of Londoner, chiefly one born in the East End of London. The traditional definition of a Cockney is that he or she was born within the sound of the Bow bells, the bells of St Mary-le-Bow, Cheapside. The sound is thought to travel as far as the City, Bethnal Green, Stepney, Shoreditch, Whitechapel, Finsbury, and all of what is now the borough of Hackney.

The first known use of the term 'Cockney' was around 1600, when Samuel Rowlands in *The Letting of Humours Blood in the Head-Vaine* referred to 'a Bow-bell Cockney'. Some seventeenth century lexicographers attempted to untangle the word, but the Oxford English Dictionary later explained that 'cockney' first meant a misshapen egg (1362), then a person ignorant of country ways (1521), and then the traditional definition of an East End Londoner. Cockneys are best known for their love of rhyming slang, where everyday words are replaced with a rhyming equivalent, such as 'Barnet Fair' for 'hair'. The rhymes are updated regularly – hence 'hair' is now 'Tony Blair'.

However, there is a lost generation of Cockneys. The bells of the church of St Mary-le-Bow were destroyed in the Blitz in 1941 and were not replaced until 1961, so for 20 years, no 'true' Cockneys were born. But really that's just splitting Tony Blairs.

QUOTE UNQUOTE

Every city has a sex and an age which have nothing to do with demography. Rome is feminine. So is Odessa. London is a teenager, an urchin, and, in this, hasn't changed since the time of Dickens. Paris, I believe, is a man in his twenties in love with an older woman.
John Berger, author and critic

RIOTING IN THE STREETS

On 6 March 1848, 10,000 people massed in Trafalgar Square to protest against the raising of income tax from three per cent to five per cent. The key speaker, a Mr Reynolds, was seized by police after he told the crowd that he would inter the king of France in Woombles Menagerie. At his arrest, the crowd turned on the police, and began to advance on St James's Park, crying 'To the Palace! Bread and revolution!' but were prevented from storming the palace when the police sealed off the route, and the would-be riot was quickly squashed.

The origin of some of London's street names

Bloomsbury Square, WC1
Bloomsbury is named after a Norman nobleman, who was given ownership of the land in this area by William the Conqueror.

Brompton Road, SW7
Once a country lane full of broom plants, the name derives from Broom-ton.

Cannon Street, EC4
Originally Candle Street, filled with candlemakers.

Cloak Lane, EC4
Open sewer street, as in the Roman's Cloaca Maxima (the Great Drain).

Gloucester Road, SW7
Once called Hogmore Lane, but renamed when the Duchess of Gloucester moved in at the beginning of the nineteenth century.

Herne Hill, SE24
Once the home of a heron or herne, as the river Effra ran through here.

Houndsditch, EC3
A ditch full of dead dogs.

King Edward Street, EC1
Once called Blowbladder Street after the fraudulent practice of inserting an animal's bladder into a dead animal and blowing it up to make it seem larger before selling it. Renamed when King Edward opened the General Post Office here.

Maiden Lane, WC2
Named after middens, which are rubbish heaps.

Newgate Street, EC1
Built in the second century, this is 'new' only in comparison to the Old Gate (Aldgate).

Pall Mall, SW1
Named after 'paille maille', a French ball and mallet game once played there.

Pudding Lane, EC3
'Pudding' in this case was not the treacle sponge kind but another word for offal.

Scotland Yard, SW1
The original Yard, Great Scotland Yard, was where the king of Scotland would stay when visiting his English counterpart.

Seven Sisters Road, N4
Named after the seven daughters of Robert the Bruce, who planted seven elm trees on Seven Sisters Road.

Spitalfields
Truncated version of Hospital Fields; a hospital first stood on this site in 1197.

Turnagain Lane, EC4
Named because of an alley that turns and goes back over the Fleet River.

DOGS IN LONDON

Where our faithful friends will sit and stay for ever more

Two bronze pointers	In the porch of St George's, Hanover Square, W1
Edith Cavell's stuffed dog	Imperial War Museum, SE1
Stone retriever	St Pancras Gardens, NW1
White greyhound	Outside, appropriately enough, The Greyhound, SW16
Appealing puppy	By the dogs' drinking fountain in Kensington Gardens, SW7
Giro	Buried in 1934, the faithful hound once owned by German ambassador Leopold von Hoesch lies in the front garden of 9 Carlton House Terrace, SW1, complete with a poignant gravestone.

QUOTE UNQUOTE

You will recognize, my boy, the first sign of age: it is when you go out into the streets of London and realize for the first time how young the policemen look.
Seymour Hicks, playwright

STEADY, VICAR

The Reverend Henry Bate (1745–1824) was as far removed from a religious man as can be imagined, and in fact for many years seemed to make his living by starting fights. While working as the editor of the *Morning Post,* he once picked a fight with a passer-by in Vauxhall Gardens for giving his female companion an inappropriate look. He insulted the stranger and challenged him to a duel. The victim roped in a friend to help, and a physical disagreement ensued in the Turk's Head Coffee House in Beak Street, which Bate won. He wrote about it in his own newspaper and was so gratified by the instant rise in circulation that he took to provoking fights with notable men, so that the resulting coverage would sell more newspapers. When one such incident backfired, Bate's proprietor, a Mr Richardson, warned him to be more careful, at which Bate accused him of spinelessness, Richardson challenged him to a duel, and Bate subsequently shot him in the arm. Bate gave up brawling for playwriting, with little success in the West End, and eventually became a London magistrate before finally retiring to Essex.

LONDON WORDS

The sullen murmur of the bees shouldering their way through the long unmown grass, or circling with monotonous insistence round the dusty gilt horns of the straggling woodbine, seemed to make the stillness more oppressive. The dim roar of London was like the bourdon note of a distant organ.

Oscar Wilde, *The Picture of Dorian Gray*

LIGHT FANTASTIC

Who turned on the Oxford Street Christmas lights?

1981	Miss World
1982	Daley Thompson
1983	Pat Phoenix
1984	Esther Rantzen
1985	Bob Geldof
1986	Den and Angie Watts (Leslie Grantham and Anita Dobson)
1987	Derek Jameson
1988	Terry Wogan
1989	Gordon Kay
1990	Cliff Richard
1991	Children from the Westminster Children's Hospital
1992	Linford Christie
1993	Richard Branson
1994	Lenny Henry
1995	The cast of Coronation Street
1996	The Spice Girls
1997	Peter Andre
1998	Zoe Ball
1999	Ronan Keating
2000	Charlotte Church
2001	S Club 7
2002	Blue
2003	Enrique Iglesias

CRIME PECULIER

In 1952 a Nigerian visitor to London was accused of committing an indecent act with a pigeon in Trafalgar Square. As the law at the time prevented only indecency with an animal, the defence attempted to put the case that a pigeon was not an animal. The judge disagreed. The accused was fined £50, and a further £10 for taking the pigeon home and eating it for dinner.

24 *Hours every day that the Heathrow Animal Reception Centre remains open throughout the year*

STRANGER THAN FICTION

When St Paul's Cathedral burned down in 1666, the only monument left standing on the site was that of the poet John Donne – who had also been Dean of St Paul's for the last 10 years of his life.

LONDON'S FIRST THEATRES

The earliest London theatres opened on the South Bank, then a seedy and dangerous place. But as theatregoing became more respectable, new playhouses began to open north of the river. These were the first:

1660 Lincoln's Inn Theatre, Portugal Street WC2
1663 Drury Lane Theatre, Drury Lane WC2
1683 Sadler's Wells, Rosebery Avenue EC1
1732 Covent Garden Theatre, Covent Garden WC2
1771 Lyceum, Wellington Street WC2
1806 Adelphi, Strand WC2: originally called the Sans Pareil
1821 Theatre Royal, Haymarket WC2
1837 Almeida, Almeida Street N1
1868 Gaiety Theatre, Strand WC2: had England's first electric lighting system in 1878

CAPITAL CONUNDRUMS

Which famous writer's portrait in the National Portrait Gallery is the only one of him known to be painted from life?
Answer on page 153.

DEATH, PLAGUES AND OTHER DISASTERS

On 3 September 1878 at 6.15pm, a ferry called the *Princess Alice* set off on her journey to London. A band played on board and the passengers danced, unaware that the captain had left the helmsman behind and replaced him with someone less experienced. So when the *Princess Alice* found herself on a collision course with the 890-ton *Bywell Castle*, no one knew what to do. The rule was to pass port to port; but another rule said that pleasure ferries should keep to the southern shoreline. The *Princess Alice* chose the latter, which put the ships starboard to starboard. Within seconds the two ships had collided, and the water was filled with terrified passengers. Some wre pulled out, but many were weighed down by their heavy Victorian clothing, and within 20 minutes of the accident, there was no one left alive to rescue. Of the estimated 750 passengers, only about 100 survived.

COLONEL THOMAS BLOOD

The seventeenth century courtier Colonel Blood was the satisfyingly named thief who attempted to steal the crown jewels in a dubious incident in 1671. Colonel Blood took a group of friends to the Tower of London, pulled out a mallet and knocked out the guard guarding the royal treasures. They seized all the treasures except the sceptre, which Blood's companions tried to cut in half to make it easier to hide, but when it proved too tough to cut, they made do with the orb and crown. However, their ineptitude was compounded when they were arrested at the main gate. The story however took a strange turn; found guilty, Blood faced torture and death; yet Charles II pardoned him and gave him a position at court and later a title and land in Ireland. The popular theory was that Charles had arranged the burglary himself, as a way of raising a bit of cash. However, it seems he might have got away with it after all; when the king died in 1687, it was found that many of the precious stones in the crown jewels had been replaced with cheap imitations.

LONDON WORDS

One day as we passed Hyde Park Corner people were streaming out of the Underground station and Lilibet said wistfully, 'Oh, dear, what fun it must be to ride in those trains.' I thought, why not? It seemed such a simple request. I asked the Duke about it that evening.

As long as we had someone with us, neither of the children's parents objected in the least. So it was arranged that the house detective should accompany us at a discreet distance, and that the Duchess's lady-in-waiting, Lady Helen Graham, should also be one of this exciting party.

Anyone would have thought we were going on an expedition to the stately pleasure domes of Kubla Khan rather than for a ride in an Underground train. The little girls bought their tickets out of their own purses. This was part of the fun. It always took them an immense time to get the money out and collect their change, and the whole business was solemn as an investiture.

...The escalator to the Underground seemed a perilous trip. Margaret's hand tightened on mine, and she swallowed apprehensively. Once safely on, down we sailed and caught our train. The little girls sat there very demurely, wide-eyed and enchanted, until suddenly at the far end of the same carriage we spotted our detective! He looked so very obviously a detective that people began to look round to try to discover what he was detecting. Mercifully, we arrived at Tottenham Court Road and got out before anyone had discovered the reason.

Marion Crawford, *The Little Princesses*

CAPITAL CONUNDRUMS

Where is London's smallest police station?
Answer on page 153.

SPORTING LONDON

The Oxford and Cambridge Boat Race was begun in 1829 when two school friends from Harrow challenged each other to a boat race: Charles Merivale and Charles Wordsworth (nephew of William), who were studying at Cambridge and Oxford respectively. The first race took place in Henley-on-Thames on 10 June 1829, and was won by Oxford (after a restart). Twenty thousand people turned out to watch, which inspired the townsfolk to begin their own annual event, the Henley Royal Regatta. The boat race relocated to Westminster in 1836, then to Putney in 1845 when Westminster became too crowded. It became an annual event in 1856, and was rowed from Putney to Mortlake.

Since then, the race has become a treasured national event, attracting enormous crowds on the riverbanks and television viewing figures of nearly nine million people. And every year's broadcast inevitably revisits the statistics of previous years, including:

- the first sinking took place in 1859, when Cambridge sank out of the race; in 1912 both crews sank and the race was re-run the following day. Oxford first sank in 1925.
- the BBC broadcast a running commentary for the first time in 1927; the race was first televised in 1938.
- in 1976, Oxford became the first team to complete the course in under 17 minutes.
- the fastest time to date was set by Cambridge in 1998, when they finished in 16 minutes and 19 seconds.
- in 1981, Sue Brown became the first woman to take part, as cox for Oxford.
- the closest finish was in 2003, when Oxford won by a mere foot; the 1877 contest was recorded as a dead heat, but the measuring equipment was unsophisticated and it is thought that Oxford in fact won by six feet.
- the current tally of wins over 150 races is Cambridge 78, Oxford 71, plus one dead heat.

QUOTE UNQUOTE

There are two places in the world where men can most effectively disappear – the city of London and the South Seas.
Herman Melville, US author

- The shortest Tube line is the Waterloo and City line, which covers just 1.5 miles.
- The longest continuous journey possible is 34 miles, from West Ruislip to Epping on the Central Line.
- The longest distance between stations is four miles between Chesham and Chalfont & Latimer on the Metropolitan line.
- The shortest distance between tube stations is 0.16 miles, the distance between Leicester Square and Covent Garden on the Piccadilly line.
- The District Line has the most stations (60) and Waterloo & City the fewest (2).
- The oldest subway line in the world is the Metropolitan line. It opened on 10 January 1863.
- The peak hour for tube suicides is 11am.
- Around half a million mice live on the Underground. No one has yet counted the rats.
- The Underground has a total of 408 escalators.
- Waterloo Station has the most escalators – 25.
- The deepest station is Hampstead at 58.5m.
- The busiest station is Victoria, which handles 7.6 million passengers a year.
- The longest escalator is at Angel, measuring 60m, rising 27.5m.
- Gladstone and Dr Barnardo were the only two people to have their coffins transported by Tube.

THE JOY OF SHEDS

Cabbies' shelters, those over-sized green sheds that can occasionally be spotted in the smarter parts of London, were first installed in the interests of road safety. On a rainy day in 1874, Captain George Armstrong, the managing editor of the *Globe* newspaper, couldn't find a cab – or, rather, he could see plenty of cabs but no cabbies. After a little investigation, he found the cab-drivers taking shelter in a nearby pub, and enjoying a beer or two. He concluded that if cabbies had their own shelters, they could enjoy cheaper food and stay away from the temptations of alcohol. Given that Victorian cabbies were notorious for their insobriety, his innovation was well overdue. He set up the Cabmen's Shelter Fund, which built 61 shelters over the next 40 years, containing tables, benches, a small kitchen and a supply of non-alcoholic drinks. Today, sadly, only 13 of these survive, but some will happily sell you a cup of tea and a bacon sandwich, whether you're a cab-driver or not.

OLD PICTURE, NEW CAPTION

*Harold was always happy to oblige the tourists with a
spirited demonstration of the Lambeth Walk*

NOW PLEASE WIPE YOUR FEET

Seven superb footscrapers to be seen in London

At **28 Meadway, NW11** – complete with horse
At **30 Chester Street** – two squatting toads
At **36A Elvaston Place** – hemispheric, double-ended and with
added finials
Outside **St Paul's at The Ridgeway, NW7** – with dolphin tails
At **12 Blenheim Road, NW8** – with dragon's wings
At **2 Cheyne Row, SW3** – a slightly disdainful face mask

LET THEM EAT CAKE

On 5 January every year, the cast and crew of the Theatre Royal Drury
Lane eat Baddeley Cake in memory of Richard Baddeley, a successful
actor. On his death in 1794, he left a sum of money in his will to provide
a cake for Twelfth Night every year, as well as wine to drink with it. So
as not to invite bad luck, the theatre still maintains the tradition, and the
cake is duly eaten every year on 5 January. It is carried into the Green
Room by attendants wearing eighteenth century costume, and the
company drinks to the health of their benefactor.

THE TRUTH ABOUT MONOPOLY

The board game that has immortalised London in a property price time-warp was not (as many Brits believe) a British game at all. Allegedly it was invented by an American called Charles Darrow in Pennsylvania in 1930 – 'allegedly' because a similar game called The Landlord Game was already in existence, patented by Elizabeth Magie in 1904. Her version differed from Darrow's game in one crucial way – it aimed to condemn property speculation, whereas Monopoly does quite the opposite.

Darrow made the first sets by hand, but when the game began to take off, he contacted a games company, Parker Brothers, to see if they would be interested in manufacturing it. They rejected it first time round, claiming that it had '52 fundamental playing errors', but after the chairman's wife stayed up till 2am playing the game, it was accepted. By 1935, it was selling at a rate of 20,000 sets a week.

Monopoly finally made the leap to London when Parker Brothers sent a set over to Waddingtons in Leeds, where the managing director gave it to his son to test. His son stayed up all night – three nights, in fact – and it was duly purchased and converted to a London-friendly version. A few changes were made to the board, but the car, the light-bulb and the policeman's hat still have a distinctly American look.

Monopoly has since gained a cult following, spawning marathons, championships, fan clubs, obsessive players and books such as Tim Moore's *Do Not Pass Go*, which the author wrote by carrying a Monopoly set around the city and rolling the dice to decide where to go next. Special editions are often created to commemorate world events, such as the 1998 World Cup Final, or to mirror cultural icons such as Disney, Star Wars, Pokemon and Coronation Street. The official website (www.monopoly.co.uk) presents some superb trivia in the form of a set of Chance cards, which throw up fascinating facts such as:

- The reigning European Monopoly champion is Gyles Brandreth.
- Monopoly became very popular in Cuba until Fidel Castro ordered that all sets be destroyed.
- Edward Heath is a keen player and was the first person to play the Russian version in the UK.
- The longest game played in a treehouse lasted 286 hours; underground 100 hours; in a bathtub 99 hours; and upside-down 36 hours.
- A £15,000 set was manufactured specially for an underwater Monopoly marathon, which lasted 1,080 hours. The board disintegrated at the end of the game.
- The longest game ever played lasted 1,680 hours, which was 70 days of continuous play.

And finally...when the current Monopoly board is updated, it has been suggested that they make things a bit more realistic by introducing a congestion charge zone, red routes, community service (instead of Go to Jail) and a player's piece shaped like a bendy bus.

Percentage more cyclists and fewer cars in central London since the congestion charge began

SIGNIFICANT STATUES

Marble Arch was designed by John Nash in 1827 to celebrate the victories at Trafalgar and Waterloo and was intended to stand in the grounds of Buckingham Palace, as an entrance arch for the royal residents. But it met with many obstacles: the foundations proved tricky; the friezes intended for its façade were put up on the Palace instead; a statue of George IV that should have sat on top ended up in Trafalgar Square; and the arch was eventually thought to be standing too close to the Palace. So it was moved to its current location, where it is stranded rather sadly on a traffic island at the far end of Oxford Street. But it has had its uses – instead of being solid, as many assume, it contains three small rooms, one at the top and two behind the sculpted panels. During the 1855 Hyde Park riots, the police used it as a hiding place, from where they took the rioters by surprise when they sprang out unexpectedly. The police continued to use it for observation purposes until 1950.

QUOTE UNQUOTE

London is a splendid place to live in for those
who can get out of it.
Lord Balfour of Burleigh, nineteenth-century Conservative MP

FERRY STRANGE

In the days before the Thames had bridges, the appropriately named William Overs was one of the many ferrymen who would row you across to the other side. Mr Overs however was no guardian angel; in fact, he was so mean that in order to save on housekeeping, he faked his own death, as mourning was usually accompanied by a day or two of fasting. Unfortunately he overestimated his family's affections, as, on hearing of his demise, they threw a party instead. To punish them, he sat up suddenly in the middle of the party, where his body had been laid out for all to see, but one alarmed guest, thinking he had risen from the dead, took one of Overs's oars and hit him over the head with it, killing him instantly. To add to the confusion, Overs's daughter Mary had sent for her boyfriend – barred from the house by her father – who rode his horse at such a reckless speed to join his lover that he fell off and was killed. Distraught, Mary spent the profits of the ferry business on founding a convent, to which was attached the Church of St Mary Overie, which is now known as Southwark Cathedral.

SEX ON STAGE

Before Mary Whitehouse was Lady Birdwood, a self-appointed moral guardian who bestowed a dubious fame upon John Bird, the writer and actor most recently seen on *The Rory Bremner Show*. In 1970, Mr Bird wrote a play called *Council of Love*, which was produced at the Criterion Theatre. The fact that God, Jesus and the Virgin Mary were represented on stage was bad enough for Lady Birdwood, but she was further outraged that the Pope was shown with his cardinals indulging in orgies with naked women during the celebration of Mass. She invoked the 1376 Blasphemy Act against Ms Fazan, the play's choreographer and the only person involved that Lady Birdwood could find to prosecute. Had she been convicted, Ms Fazan could, according to the law, have been burned as a white witch. Fortunately the court felt that she could not be held responsible and the case was dismissed.

LONDON WORDS

London, thou art of townes *A per se*.
Soveraign of cities, semeliest in sight,
Of high renoun, riches, and royaltie;
Of lordis, barons, and many goodly knyght;
Of most delectable lusty ladies bright;
Of famous prelatis in habitis clericall;
Of merchauntis full of substaunce and myght:
London, thou art the flour of Cities all
William Dunbar, *To the City of London*

TOWERING FACTS

- The Tower of London was built by William the Conqueror in the eleventh century.
- Its original English name was the White Tower from the Celtic Bryn Gwyn; 'gwyn' means white or pure, 'bryn' means hill.
- The Tower was built on an ancient site, where a sacred mound once stood.
- It was believed that two former British kings were buried under the mound: Brutus (the reputed founder of London) in 1100 BC and Molmutius, buried around 500 BC.
- Malory, in *Le Morte D'Arthur*, says that Guinevere took refuge here to avoid marriage to Sir Mordred.
- It is thought that a 150-foot Roman well sits beneath the Tower, possibly built for astronomical observations, as the deep hole cuts out any glare from the moon.
- The round turret at the north-east corner of the White Tower was used as an observatory until the seventeenth century.

LONDON, WHERE?

A few US towns that sound familiar...

London, *Arkansas*
London, *Arizona*
London, *California*
London, *Kentucky*
New London, *Minnesota*
New London, *Missouri*
New London, *New Hampshire*
New London, *North Carolina*
London, *Ohio*
London, *Oregon*
New London, *Pennsylvania*
London, *Texas*
London, *West Virginia*

RIOTING IN THE STREETS

The first Bloody Sunday took place on 13 November 1887, when the Social Democratic Federation organised a meeting in Trafalgar Square to protest against the government's policies. The police were ordered to stop the demonstration, and advanced on the crowd. Onlookers were shocked at the police violence. One commented: 'To keep a crowd moving is, I believe, a technical term for the process of riding roughshod in all directions, scattering, frightening and batoning the people.' Two people were killed and 200 were injured.

THE TREE OF LIFE

While the government was squandering squillions on the Millennium Dome, the new century was being commemorated in a much simpler and more meaningful way by the planting of a tree. A small sapling was planted in the churchyard of Chelsea Old Church in November 2000 to celebrate the birth of Christ – which seems simple enough, but there the plot thickens. It is a piece of Glastonbury Thorn, the legendary tree of Glastonbury, which is supposed to have grown from the staff of Joseph of Arimathea, who planted it in the ground when he landed in Britain with the Holy Grail. The original tree was cut down in a Puritan raid, but a cutting was kept by a priest and replanted. The Queen is sent a cutting at Christmas each year to decorate her Christmas table. Sadly for Chelsea Old Church, despite much care and attention, the Thorn failed to take root. We can only assume that it fell on stony ground.

IT BEATS AS IT SWEEPS AS IT CLEANS

The invention of the vacuum-cleaner came about when a young man named H Cecil Booth witnessed a carpet-cleaning demonstration at an exhibition at London's Empire Music Hall in 1898. Booth watched as a US invention blew dust messily into a box, and he suggested that it might be better if the contraption sucked up the dust. The demonstrator said it couldn't be done – so Booth set out to do it. After experimenting with bits of fabric, through which he sucked up dust from his own carpet, by mouth, Booth found that a closely woven handkerchief worked best. He duly invented a suction cleaner that filtered out the dust, which he patented in 1901. One of the first buildings in the world to be vacuumed clean was Westminster Abbey, which Booth was employed to tidy up for Edward VII's coronation. Years of historic dust were duly removed, to the astonishment of the Abbey's cleaning staff. Booth's machines were also used to clean the dust from Crystal Palace, where an outbreak of spotted fever was being blamed on infected dust particles. Fifteen machines stripped the building of every last scrap of dust, and the outbreak was quashed. Versions of the machine were developed in Europe and, most famously, in the US by a Mr Spangler, who sold the rights to his invention to one William Hoover. Despite the fact that no one now remembers Cecil Booth, it is perhaps just as well; 'I'll run a Booth over it,' doesn't sound quite the same.

QUOTE UNQUOTE

The marvellous maturity of London! I would rather be dead in this town than preening my feathers in heaven.
Nicholas Monsarrat, novelist

LONDON LEGENDS

Norman Balon is the celebrated landlord of the Coach and Horses in Soho, the favourite drinking-place of the late Jeffrey Barnard, and the meeting place for *Private Eye* and the *Oldie*. His unique selling-points are his irascibility and intolerance for customers who fall short of his exacting standards, who are ejected from the pub without ceremony. This is not, however, the result of his drinking his own profits, as he is a teetotaller. When described as 'crapulous' by an unsuspecting author, who implied that he was in a sorry and drunken state, he sued for libel and the book was withdrawn. Though it has to be said that it did little to improve his mood.

Sir Charles Barry (1795–1860): Houses of Parliament, Travellers Club in Pall Mall, Reform Club

Edward Middleton Barry (1830–1880): completed his father's work on the Houses of Parliament

Sir William Chambers (1723–1796): Kew Gardens pagoda, Somerset House (1776)

Norman, Lord Foster (1935–): British Museum Great Court, HSBC HQ at Canary Wharf, No.1 London Wall, Tower Place, Canary Wharf station, Sir Alexander Fleming Building at Imperial College, Swiss Re HQ ('The Gherkin'), Millennium Bridge, City Hall

Nicholas Hawksmoor (1661–1736): St George's Church in Bloomsbury, Christ Church in Spitalfields.

James Gibbs (1682–1754): St Martin-in-the-Fields (1726)

Inigo Jones (1573-1652): Queen's House at Greenwich; rebuilt the Banqueting Hall, parts of old St Paul's (before 1666), the Queen's Chapel at Marlborough House

Sir Denys Louis Lasdun (1914–2001): Royal College of Physicians, National Theatre, Hallfield Estate, Keeling House

Sir Edwin Landseer Lutyens (1869–1944): Cenotaph, Whitehall, the Grosvenor Estate

John Nash (1752–1835): Marble Arch, Regent Street, recreated Buckingham Palace from Buckingham House

Sir Joseph Paxton (1801–1865): Great Exhibition Building of 1851, Crystal Palace

Sir John Soane (1753–1837): Bank of England, Dulwich Picture Gallery, Sir John Soane Museum

Sir Robert Smirke (1781–1867): Covent Garden Theatre, British Museum, King's College, Royal College of Physicians

Sir George Gilbert Scott (1811–1878): Albert Memorial, St Pancras

Norman Shaw (1831–1912): Old Swan House, Chelsea, New Scotland Yard, Gaiety Theatre, Aldwych, Piccadilly Hotel

Sir John Wolfe-Barry (1836–1918): Tower Bridge

Lord Richard Rogers (1933–): Lloyd's Building, Millennium Dome

Sir Christopher Wren (1632–1723): 51 London churches, including St Paul's (rebuilt after 1666), Chelsea Hospital, Greenwich Observatory, parts of Hampton Court Palace and the Royal Naval College, St Clement Dane in the Strand, St James in Piccadilly, St Mary le Bow in Cheapside.

The Pheasants' Revolt

CAPITAL CONUNDRUMS

What is the colour of a banana and
the shape of an orange?
Answer on page 153.

36 *Year in the 1900s in which the first television broadcast was made, from
Alexandra Palace*

QUOTE UNQUOTE

This melancholy London – I sometimes imagine that the souls of the lost are compelled to walk through its streets perpetually. One feels them passing like a whiff of air.
WB Yeats, poet

MODERN TALES OF LONDON

City of Spades, Colin McCabe (1957)
Absolute Beginners, Colin McCabe (1959)
Mr Love and Justice, Colin McCabe (1960)
Sour Sweet, Timothy Mo (1982)
Money, Martin Amis (1984)
London Fields, Martin Amis (1989)
The Buddha of Suburbia, Hanif Kureishi (1990)
Fever Pitch, Nick Hornby (1992)
Hawksmoor, Peter Ackroyd (1993)
Downriver, Iain Sinclair (1995)
While England Sleeps, David Leavitt (1995)
Grey Area, Will Self (1996)
High Fidelity, Nick Hornby (1996)
Lights Out for the Territory, Iain Sinclair (1997)
Metroland, Julian Barnes (1997)
Armadillo, William Boyd (1998)
Capital, Maureen Duffy (2001)
White Teeth, Zadie Smith (2001)
The Bat Tattoo, Russell Hoban (2002)
Fingersmith, Sarah Waters (2002)
Brick Lane, Monica Ali (2004)

LONDON WORDS

Everything in this monster city interests me. People here seem always to express distances by parables. To a stranger it is just a little confusing to be so parabolic – so to speak. I collar a citizen, and I think I am going to get some valuable information out of him. I ask him how far it is to Birmingham, and he says it is 21 shillings and six-pence. Now we know that doesn't help a man who is trying to learn. I find myself downtown somewhere, and I want to get some sort of idea where I am – being usually lost when alone – and I stop a citizen and say: 'How far is it to Charing Cross?' 'Shilling fare in a cab,' and off he goes. I suppose if I were to ask a Londoner how far it is from the sublime to the ridiculous, he would try to express it in coin.
Mark Twain, *addressing the Savage Club in London in 1872*

London's bridges, in order of appearance, from east to west

Name	Type	Date first opened
Queen Elizabeth II	road	1991
Tower	road	1894
London	road	1831
Alexandra	rail	1866
Southwark	road	1819
Millennium	foot	2000
Blackfriars	rail	1864
Blackfriars	road	1769
Waterloo	road	1817
Hungerford	rail and foot	1863
Westminster	road	1750
Lambeth	road	1862
Vauxhall	road	1816
Grosvenor	rail	1860
Chelsea	road	1934
Albert	road	1873
Battersea	road	1772
Battersea	rail	1863
Wandsworth	road	1873
Putney	rail	1889
Putney	road	1729
Hammersmith	road	1827
Barnes	rail and foot	1849
Chiswick	road	1933
Kew	rail	1869
Kew	road	1759
Richmond Lock	foot	1894
Twickenham	road	1933
Richmond	rail	1848
Richmond	road	1777
Teddington Lock	foot	1889
Kingston	road	1828
Hampton Court	road	1753

LAST TO GO

The last beheading to take place at the Tower of London was of Simon Fraser, Lord Lovat in 1747. The last execution was of German spy Josef Jakobs, who faced a firing squad on 15 August 1941. His execution chair is now in a museum in Leeds, but, according to one of the tour guides, before it was moved, his relatives paid a visit and took a snap of his grandchildren sitting in the chair in which he was shot.

38 *Year in the 1900s when the Wembley Cup Final became the first football match to be broadcast live*

PUB QUIZ

Who drank here?

Holly Bush, Holly Mount NW3
Customers: Samuel Johnson, Charles Lamb

The Angel, Bermondsey Wall SE16
Customers: Samuel Pepys, Captain Cook

Fitzroy Tavern, Charlotte Street
Customers: George Orwell, Thornton Wilder, Dylan Thomas, Cyril Connolly

Museum Tavern, Great Russell Street, WC1
Customers: Karl Marx and Dylan Thomas

Seven Stars, Carey Street WC2
Early seventeenth century, one of the smallest in London. Charles Dickens drank here.

The Dagger, Aldersgate
Customer: Ben Jonson (as mentioned in *The Alchemist*)

Spaniard's Inn, Spaniard's Road NW3
Customers: Percy Bysshe Shelley, John Keats, Lord Byron, Charles Dickens. Dick Turpin stayed here and there is a dedicated Dick Turpin room.

Prospect of Whitby, Wapping Wall, E1
Dates back to time of Henry VIII; customers included Samuel Pepys, Rex Whistler, Judge Jeffries and a variety of thieves and smugglers

Assembly House, Kentish Town Road NW5
Customer: TS Eliot

LONDON WORDS

RESPIRATOR, *n*. An apparatus fitted over the nose and mouth of an inhabitant of London, whereby to filter the visible universe in its passage to the lungs.

Ambrose Bierce, *The Devil's Dictionary*

LEFT LUGGAGE

In October 1953, Dylan Thomas left his handwritten manuscript – the only copy – for *Under Milk Wood* in the Admiral Duncan pub on Old Compton Street in Soho shortly before he left the country, promising that whoever found it could keep it. His promise sparked off a bizarre treasure hunt, and the manuscript was eventually tracked down by BBC producer Douglas Cleverdon, who later sold it for £2,000. It is unfortunate that the Admiral Duncan is more likely to be remembered for another parcel that was left there in April 1999, a nail bomb, which exploded under a table, killing three people and injuring many more.

ROYAL TOMBS IN WESTMINSTER ABBEY

Elizabeth I • Mary I • Edward the Confessor
Henry VII • James I • Edward VI
George II • Henry III • Edward I
Edward III • Richard II • Henry V
Anne • Charles II • William III
Mary II • Mary Stewart

A LONDON FIRST

Dulwich Picture Gallery was the first public art gallery in Britain.
Its collection was compiled by Sir Francis Bourgeois and Noël
Desenfans at the request of the King of Poland. However, when
Poland was taken over by Russian and Prussian forces, the king
abdicated, leaving Bourgeois and Desenfans with a formidable
collection of art but nowhere to exhibit it. Both the British
government and the British Museum declined to buy the paintings.
Desenfans died in 1807 before the problem was resolved, so when
Bourgeois died in 1811 he left the paintings to Dulwich College.
His will decreed that they should be accessible to the public, and
the Dulwich Picture Gallery was duly founded in the same year to
carry out his request. Both Desenfans and Bourgeois are entombed
in sarcophagi in the centre of the gallery.

PATRON SAINTS OF LONDON

A few patron saints that might be needed in London

Actors	*St Genesius, St Vitus*
Architects	*St Thomas, St Barbara*
Bankers	*St Matthew*
Beggars	*St Martin of Tours*
Broadcasters	*Angel Gabriel*
Cab drivers	*St Fiacre*
Civil servants	*Thomas More*
Editors	*St John Bosco*
Hoteliers	*St Gentian, St Amand*
Innkeepers	*St Amand, St Martin of Tours, St Gentian*
Journalists	*St Francis of Sales*
Judges	*St John of Capistrano*
Lawyers	*St Genesius, St Ivo, Thomas More*
Lost articles	*St Anthony of Padua*
Messengers	*Angel Gabriel*
Politicians	*Thomas More*
Tax collectors	*St Matthew*

YOU SAW IT HERE FIRST

The first daily newspaper in the English language and the world's oldest continuously published newspaper was the *London Gazette*. It was first published on 7 November 1665, and is still published today, nearly 340 years later. It was first called the *Oxford Gazette*, as the court had retired to London to escape the plague, but when they returned to the capital, the paper went with them and was renamed. Samuel Pepys noted its introduction in his diary:

This day the first of the 'Oxford Gazettes' came out, which is very pretty, full of news, and no folly in it.

The paper provided a mixture of government notices, trade news, business news, shipping reports and notices about royal appointments. Historic events were recorded, such as the Great Fire of London, the Battle of Waterloo and the declaration of war against Germany in 1939. Today, the *London Gazette* is published each weekday by HMSO (Her Majesty's Stationery Office), and contains such things as national statistics, legal developments and innovations, changes in state legislation, summaries of events in the Houses of Parliament, information on European government and legislation and notices of personal and corporate insolvency (which are usually the largest categories). It also carries supplements on certain occasions, such as law exam results, the Royal honours lists and Premium Bond prize draw details. Now available online, it still carries the original, slightly stern strapline: 'Published by Authority'.

RIOTING IN THE STREETS

Black Monday was the name given to 8 February 1886, when workers made redundant by the closure of the sugar refineries gathered in Trafalgar Square to protest. The protest was backed by the Conservative Association, but taken over by the Social-Democratic Federation. Ten thousand people marched along Pall Mall and threw objects at the Reform Club, as its members appeared at the windows to see what was going on. The SDF leaders were prosecuted but acquitted, but the march put London into a state of chaos for several weeks.

ALAS, POOR EMANUEL...

In March 1978, Sotheby's of London auctioned the skull of Swedish scientist and mystic Emanuel Swedenborg, which went to a Swedish bidder for $3,200. The skull had been stolen by an amateur phrenologist, then turned up a century after Swedenborg's death in an antique shop in Wales, where it was bought by one of his heirs before being offered for auction.

LONDON'S BURNING

London's first major fire was in AD 60, when the warrior queen Boadicea burned the city to the ground. Boadicea was the queen of the Iceni, the tribe that occupied East Anglia, but which was under Roman jurisdiction, and subject to conscription and heavy taxes. When Boadicea's husband, King Prasutagus, died, he left most of his wealth and estate to the Emperor Nero, but retained a small part of it for his wife and two daughters. But the Romans decided to take all of it, and when Boadicea protested, they took her prisoner and flogged her and raped her two daughters. The women escaped and returned to their home, and had soon raised an army of over 100,000 men and women to avenge the Queen's treatment and reclaim England from the Romans. They marched in turn on Colchester, London and St Alban's, Roman strongholds at the time, and burned the last two to the ground. The fires in London were so fierce and reached such high temperatures that they left, buried deep beneath a part of the City, a geological layer known as Boadicea's Layer, a chunk of red band of fired clay and debris.

Boadicea was not merciful; any Britons loyal to the Romans met a horrible and bloody end. The warrior queen and her armies defeated the Romans in several confrontations, but were eventually beaten on the island of Anglesey, in a battle in which over 80,000 Britons were slaughtered. Boadicea survived the battle but chose to poison herself rather than fall into the hands of the Romans. A bronze statue of her stands on Victoria Embankment, erected in 1850 as a memorial to the exceptional warrior queen.

LONDON WORDS

During the summer months milk is sold in Smithfield, Billingsgate, and other markets, and on Sundays in Battersea-fields, Clapham-common, Camberwell-green, Hampstead-heath, and similar places. About twenty men are engaged in this sale. They usually wear a smock frock, and have the cans and yoke used by the regular milk-sellers; they are not itinerant. The skim milk – for they sell none else – is purchased at the dairies at 1 1/2 d. a quart, and even the skim milk is also further watered by the street-sellers. Their cry is 'Half-penny half-pint! Milk! The tin measure however in which the milk-and-water is served is generally a 'slang', and contains but half of the quantity proclaimed. The purchasers are chiefly boys and children; rarely men, and never costermongers, I was told, 'for they reckon milk sickly'.

Henry Mayhew, *Mayhew's London*

42 *Year in 1800s in which the Scissors, Paper, Stone club was founded in London*

OLD PICTURE, NEW CAPTION

*An unsuspecting tourist discovers how much it will
cost to be driven south of the river*

MONET IN LONDON

Paintings of London by Claude Monet
Houses of Parliament, London 1905
Sun Breaking Through the Fog, Houses of Parliament, London 1904
The London Harbour
Houses of Parliament at Sunset, London, 1903
The Waterloo Bridge, London 1903
Waterloo Bridge at Dusk, London 1904
Waterloo Bridge at Sunset, London,1904

I'M PUTTING ON MY TOP HAT

In January 1797, hatter John Etherington caused a public disturbance
by wearing a hat of his own design outside his shop on the Strand.
The sight of him modelling his tall, cylindrical creation drew such a
large crowd that one spectator was accidentally pushed through a
shop window and Etherington was arrested. However, the event drew
the right kind of attention and the hat caught on, and Etherington's
top hat soon became all the rage.

The year AD in which the Romans established the city of Londinium 43

INMATES OF NEWGATE PRISON

Moll Cutpurse (Mary Frith), highwaywoman
Daniel Defoe, author, for publishing a satirical pamphlet
Sir Thomas Malory, author of *Le Morte d'Arthur*, for murder
Titus Oates, imprisoned for falsely claiming that there was a
Catholic plot to assassinate Charles II
Jack Sheppard, burglar, immortalised in The Beggar's Opera
Jonathan Wild, Thief-Taker, for being over-zealous in his duties

LONG MEG

Long Meg of Westminster was supposedly a formidably tall and bawdy woman whose deeds became the subject of ballads and pamphlets, and were even made into a comic play performed in London in 1595. Described by some as 'a lower-class roaring-girl', she joined in the fashion for cross-dressing, which brought condemnation down upon her head from the king and his churchmen, alarmed perhaps by such early stirrings of feminism.

In Captain Grose's *Dictionary of the Vulgar Tongue*, Meg's nickname was 'a jeering name for a tall woman', and she is mentioned in another book, *The Sword Through the Centuries,* as having vanquished a Spanish knight with her sword and buckler. However, some historians doubt that she was an actual person, and she may have existed only in folklore. Her name has since been given to several objects of unusual size: the large blue-black marble in the south cloister of Westminster Abbey, over the grave of Gervasius de Blois, is called 'Long Meg of Westminster', and her name also refers to a gun in the Tower of London. And the *Edinburgh Antiquarian Magazine* in September 1769 wrote of a Peter Branan, aged 104, who was 6ft 6in tall and was commonly called Long Meg of Westminster.

We can also only assume that, if she did exist, being called Long Meg rather than Tall Meg had a certain significance.

THE HOUSE THAT WASN'T

In Leinster Terrace W2 is a Victorian terrace frontage with windows, a door… and nothing else. It is a beautiful piece of trompe l'oeil measuring 18 inches thick, which was built to disguise a huge air-vent space behind it, part of the Tube network. In a famous hoax of the 1930s, a sharp-eyed conman made himself a quick fortune by selling 10 guinea tickets for a charity ball to be held at the address to hundreds of excited guests, who duly turned up in evening dress and were baffled to get no response when they knocked at the door.

DEADLY VERSE

Ring-a-ring o' roses
A pocket full of posies,
A-tishoo! A-tishoo!
We all fall down.

The nursery rhyme of Ring-a-Ring o' Roses is more of a death knell than a happy verse. It commemorates, in charming euphemisms, the Great Plague of London, which broke out in 1664. The ring of roses is the circular rash that was one of the symptoms; the pocket full of posies refers to the bunches of herbs that people carried to ward off the germs; and the sneezing is the fatal sneeze which many victims suffered just before their final and fatal collapse.

WHAT AN EXHIBITION

The highest attendance figures at London's museums

Exhibition	Where	When	Attendance
Treasures of Tutankhamun	British Museum	1972-3	1,694,117
Britain Can Make It	Victoria & Albert	1946	1,500,000
Spanish Art Treasures	Victoria & Albert	1881	1,022,000
Monet in the 20th century	Royal Academy	1999	813,000
The Genius of China	Royal Academy	1973-4	771,000
Pompeii AD 79	Royal Academy	1976	633,000
Turner Watercolours	British Museum	1973	585,046
The Great Japan Exhibition	Royal Academy	1982	523,000
Matisse, Picasso	Tate Modern	2002	467,166
The Vikings	British Museum	1980	465,000
The Aztecs	Royal Academy	2002-3	465,000
Thracian Treasures	British Museum	1976	424,465
Cezanne	Tate Britain	1996	406,688

LONDON WORDS

What an amazing thing is the coming of spring to London. The very pavements seem ready to crack and lift under the denied earth; in the air is a consciousness of life which tells you that if traffic stopped for a fortnight grass would grow again in Piccadilly and corn would spring in pavement cracks where a horse had spilt his 'feed'. And the squares of London, so dingy and black since the first October gale, fill week by week with the rising tide of life, just as the sea, running up the creeks and pushing itself forward inch by inch towards the land, comes at last to each remote rock pool.

HV Morton, *In Search of England*

SPIRITS IN THE SKY

A man named Thomas Willson came up with an idea in 1829 that he thought would solve London's chronically congested graveyards; build a burial pyramid. His plans showed a construction that would stand taller than today's Canary Wharf and would hold five million dead bodies. The burial sites on each of his pyramid's 94 floors would be reached by steam-powered lifts. His scheme was not taken up by the government of the day, who opted for the more British way of burying their dead – underground and out of sight.

LONDON ON LOCATION

Films shot in the British Museum

Blackmail (1929): the finale was set in – and on the roof of – the British Museum

Night of the Demon (1957): supernatural forces take over the reading room

Arabesque (1966): Gregory Peck and Sophia Loren visit the museum

Isadora (1968): the heroine is entranced by the Elgin Marbles

The Day of the Jackal (1973): Edward Fox does some research in the reading room

The Awakening (1980): Charlton Heston reawakens an evil princess in the Hall of Egyptian Antiquities

Maurice (1987): features the Assyrian Salon

Born Romantic (2000): Jane Horrocks admires the Elgin Marbles

The Mummy Returns (2001): Brendan Fraser and Rachel Weisz escape four evil mummies by jumping on a double-decker bus outside the Museum (the interior shots were shot in a studio)

Possession (2002): Gwyneth Paltrow and Aaron Eckhart research their dead Victorian poets in the museum

A STRETCHER THE IMAGINATION

Some of London's railings have more to them than meets the eye. About six feet long and four feet wide, each panel consists of a close metal mesh and, near each corner, the outer rail has been bent outwards in a shallow V-shape. The simple explanation is that these were primitive stretchers used in World War Two – the V-shapes acted as the feet when the stretchers were set down on the ground. The war over, they were used to make fences, as raw materials for rebuilding were, by then, very thin on the ground.

46 *Year in the 1700s when a survey showed there was one tavern to every five houses in London*

A few phobias that might keep you out of the city

Acousticophobia ....Fear of loud noises
Agoraphobia ....Fear of open spaces or of being in crowded,
public places or leaving a safe place
Amathophobia ....Fear of dust
Anthropophobia or *Sociophobia* ....Fear of people or society
Aphenphosmphobia ....Fear of being touched
Automysophobia ....Fear of being dirty
Bacteriophobia ....Fear of bacteria
Batophobia ....Fear of heights or being close to high buildings
Enochlophobia ....Fear of crowds
Hodophobia ....Fear of road travel
Kainophobia ....Fear of anything new
Mechanophobia ....Fear of machines
Ophthalmophobia ....Fear of being stared at
Ornithophobia ....Fear of birds
Phengophobia ....Fear of daylight
Potamophobia ....Fear of rivers or running water
Siderodromophobia ....Fear of trains or train travel
Stenophobia ....Fear of narrow things or places
Suriphobia ....Fear of mice
Xenophobia ....Fear of strangers or foreigners

QUOTE UNQUOTE

When it's three o'clock in New York, it's still 1938 in London.
Bette Midler, actress

RIOTING IN THE STREETS

On 22 September 1831, the House of Commons introduced the Reform Bill in an attempt to abolish 'rotten boroughs', parliamentary constituencies that had very few voters but still had the power to elect members to the House of Commons. This meant that candidates could easily bribe or cheat their way into power. The Tories were also set against increasing the number of people who were entitled to vote. The House of Commons passed the Reform Bill, but it was defeated by the Tory-dominated House of Lords. When the news broke, there were riots in several British towns, including in London, where the houses owned by the Duke of Wellington and bishops who had voted against the Bill in the Lords were attacked. Finally, on 13 April 1832, the Reform Act was passed by a small majority in the House of Lords.

London Stone in Cannon Street is an ancient relic of uncertain history. In fact, its most notable claim to fame is that no one really knows where it came from. The many theories include:

- It is over 3,000 years old, and possibly part of a pagan altar
- It is located along a ley line connecting significant places, such as St Paul's and Tower Hill
- It is the mystical central point of London, and possibly of Britain
- It is a piece of the altar of the temple of Diana, built by Brutus of Troy when he settled in Britain after fleeing the destruction of Troy
- It is a piece from an ancient stone circle that once stood on Ludgate Hill, on the site of the current St Paul's
- It is part of the wall built by the Romans
- It was the point from which the Romans measured all distances in London
- It is a Saxon ceremonial stone
- It is the stone from which King Arthur pulled his sword

The first written reference to the London Stone is in an early tenth century book belonging to Athelstan, King of the West Saxons, which described buildings as being 'near unto London stone'.

It was referred to on late twelfth century maps as Lonenstane or Londenstane. People who lived nearby were called de Londenstane, and the first mayor of London was Henry Fitzailwyn de Londonestone.

The London Stone became the traditional place to pass laws, make proclamations, reclaim debts and swear oaths, often in front of a crowd. Petitioners could strike the Stone with their papers in order to make their position known to the authorities.

When Jack Cade, led a rebellion against King Henry VI to protest about crippling taxes and royal corruption, he led his followers into London and stopped at the London Stone to strike it with his sword and declare himself Lord Mayor. The event was captured in *Henry VI Part Two*.

The stone originally stood in the middle of Cannon Street, but was moved in 1742 and placed against the wall of St Swithin's Church. It was then removed in 1798, but when local residents protested, it was embedded in the wall of the church to keep it out of the way. In 1940, the church was destroyed by bombs, but the stone was unharmed. It was removed to the Guildhall Museum for safekeeping, and when the church was demolished in 1960, it was replaced in the wall of the building constructed on that site.

Now set into the wall of the offices for the Overseas-Chinese Banking Corporation, it appears to be an insignificant piece of oolite, which is the only known remnant of the original stone. An application to move the Stone once more was approved on 10 July 2002 and it is due to be set into the wall of a proposed new building on the same site.

CAPITAL CONUNDRUMS

Who buried his wine and a Parmesan cheese in his garden, to save them from the Great Fire of London?
Answer on page 153.

FLESH, FISH AND FOWL ROADS

A menagerie of London road names

Albacore Crescent, *SE13*
Badger Court, *NW2*
Camel Road, *E16*
Dog Lane, *NW10*
Elephant Lane, *SE16*
Fish Street Hill, *EC3*
Goat House Bridge, *SE25*
Hare Street, *SE18*
Ibis Lane, *W4*
Jay Mews, *SW7*
Kingfisher Avenue, *E11*
Lamb Street, *E1*
Magpie Close, *NW9*
Nightingale Lane, *SW12*
Oyster Row, *E1*
Pelican Stairs, *E1*
Rabbit Row, *W8*
Sheep Lane, *E8*
Three Colts Lane, *E2*
Unicorn Buildings, *E1*
Wagtail Close, *NW9*

YOU LIVE... WHERE?

While residents may occasionally be baffled by the names given to roads in London, they should be grateful they did not live there in the thirteenth century. Back in 1230, Grub Street was known as Grope Lane, which in turn was a shortened version of its full and rather too literal title of 'Gropecuntelane'. The reason was that the street was part of the Southwark red-light district, otherwise known as the 'stews'. This street name was in fact found in several British cities at the time, although out of sensitivity for the gentle reader the remaining examples have not been listed here. Enquire at your local library. However, similarly named streets have been renamed Magpie Lane in Oxford, Host Street in Bristol and Grape Street in York, which is much nicer.

COCKNEY LONDON

A few London place names and their Cockney meanings

Boat Race .... *face*
Chalk Farm .... *arm*
Conan Doyle .... *boil*
Daily Mail .... *tale*
Doctor Crippen .... *dripping*
Duke of York .... *chalk, cork or fork*
Hampstead Heath .... *teeth*
Harvey Nichols .... *pickles*
Jack the Ripper .... *kipper*
Lord Mayor .... *swear*
Newington Butts .... *guts*
Richard the Third .... *bird*

CLASSIC LONDON TALES

A Journal of the Plague Year, Daniel Defoe (1722)
Oliver Twist, Charles Dickens (1838)
The Old Curiosity Shop, Charles Dickens (1840)
Little Dorrit, Charles Dickens (1857)
Our Mutual Friend, Charles Dickens (1865)
The Europeans, Henry James (1878)
Daisy Miller, Henry James (1879)
Liza of Lambeth, Somerset Maugham (1897)
Hangover Square, Patrick Hamilton (1941)
The Heat of the Day, Elizabeth Bowen (1949)
The End of the Affair, Graham Greene (1951)
The Naked Civil Servant, Quentin Crisp (1968)
The Four-Gated City, Doris Lessing (1969)

TOP TEN TOWERS

The ten tallest towers in London

One Canada Square	50 floors	244m	800ft
8 Canada Square	45 floors	200m	655ft
25 Canada Square	45 floors	200m	655ft
Telecom Tower	43 floors	191m	625ft (inc mast)
Tower 42	43 floors	183m	600ft
30 St Mary Axe ('The Gherkin')	41 floors	180m	590ft
One Churchill Place, E14	33 floors	156m	513ft (due 2004)
25 Bank Street, E14	33 floors	153m	502ft
40 Bank Street, E14	33 floors	153m	502ft
10 Upper Bank Street, E14	32 floors	151m	495ft

50 *Millions of visitors who go Christmas shopping in Regent Street every year*

TILL DEATH US DO PART?

When the first wife of Martin van Butchell died in 1775, van Butchell declined to bury his poor wife and instead had her embalmed, fitted with glass eyes and displayed, wearing her wedding dress, in a glass case at his home in Mayfair. But unless this be mistaken for an act of love by a husband who could not bear to be parted from his wife, it should be noted that her considerable fortune was bequeathed to a distant relative, to be paid as soon as she was 'dead and buried'. Van Butchell also charged visitors to see her body. In 1815 after van Butchell's death, his son donated the embalmed body to the Royal College of Surgeons, where it was eventually destroyed by a German bomb in 1941.

LONDON WORDS

Earth has not anything to show more fair:
Dull would he be of soul who could pass by
A sight so touching in its majesty:
This City now doth, like a garment, wear
The beauty of the morning; silent, bare,
Ships, towers, domes, theatres, and temples lie
Open unto the fields, and to the sky;
All bright and glittering in the smokeless air.
Never did sun more beautifully steep
In his first splendour, valley, rock or hill;
Ne'er saw I, never felt, a calm so deep!
The river glideth at his own sweet will:
Dear God! the very houses seem asleep;
And all that mighty heart is lying still!

William Wordsworth, *Westminster Bridge*

QUOTE UNQUOTE

*Tis said, London and New York take the
nonsense out of a man.*
Ralph Waldo Emerson, US writer and philosopher

IT SPOILS ONE'S VIEW

Until 1954, it was forbidden for a building to be taller than the width of the street that it was on, which some ascribe to the fact that Queen Victoria's view from Buckingham Palace had been obscured by a 14-storey hotel, to her considerable fury. However, the result was that many roads were made wider – hence the vast expanse of roads such as Northumberland Avenue, just a short stroll from the Palace.

CAPITAL CONUNDRUMS

Which tube line describes its entire function most accurately?
Answer on page 153.

THE LONDON GROUP

Formerly known as the Fitzroy Group and the Camden Town Group, the London Group, formed by Walter Sickert, brought together many major painters of the era

Robert Bevan	1865–1925	*English*
Jacob Epstein	1880–1959	*American (became British)*
Harold Gilman	1876–1919	*British*
Charles Isaac Ginner	1878–1952	*French*
Spencer Gore	1878–1914	*English*
Duncan Grant	1885–1978	*English*
Augustus John	1878–1961	*British*
Wyndham Lewis	1882–1957	*Canadian/British Writer/Painter*
Henry Lamb	1883–1960	*English*
James Bolivar Manson	1879–1945	*British*
Lucien Pissarro	1863–1944	*French*
Walter Richard Sickert	1860–1942	*British*

LONDON'S BURNING

In the Middle Ages, the amount of tax that a person had paid was recorded on a tally stick, in which notches were made for each payment. The stick was then split in half lengthways, and the government kept the other identically notched half, as a record – an early tax receipt. The government's halves were piled up over the centuries in the Palace of Westminster, as no one knew what else to do with them. It wasn't until 1834 that someone suggested they could perhaps be got rid of. They were duly burned in a furnace under the House of Lords, but unfortunately the furnace was overloaded and then left to burn unsupervised. It quickly set fire to the rest of the tally sticks and burned down most of the Palace. It also destroyed some historic documents, such as the warrant for the execution of Charles I. The event was immortalised in Turner's painting, 'The Burning of the Houses of Parliament'. *The Times* reported a sense of subdued sadness among the near-silent spectators, excepting one who described it as 'Certainly the grandest thing we have ever witnessed'.

52 *Year in the 1900s when London's last tram ran – before they began again in Croydon in 2000*

While he agreed the traffic in central London was bad, George thought the new trams were taking things a step too far

THE REAL LONDON BRIDGE

Various wooden bridges have stood on or near the site of the current London Bridge since before Roman times, but in 1176 a cleric called Peter de Colechurch, decided to build a revolutionary stone bridge. It took 33 years to build, and consisted of 19 arches, which stretched 900 feet across the Thames. It was paid for by a tax levied by Henry II on wool, which gave rise to the saying 'London Bridge was built upon woolpacks'.

Peter de Colechurch died before the bridge was completed, and was suitably buried in the crypt contained within the bridge. But his pioneering bridge stood for 655 years before it was defeated by the growing volume of London traffic, and demolished to make way for a bigger, stronger construction. However, its successor, designed by John Rennie lasted only 140 years before it had to be replaced again, thanks once more to the pressures of traffic and population. An arch of the original wooden bridge could be found in the Museum of London, and an arch of the Rennie Bridge lives in Kew Gardens. Two of the stone structures that were on the bridge were displayed in Victoria Park, Hackney, by St Augustine's Gate.

Proof that London Underground drivers have a heart, a soul and a sense of humour. In spite of everything.

Northern Line: 'Hello, this is the driver speaking, I am the captain of your train, and we will be departing shortly. We will be cruising at an altitude of approximately zero feet, and our scheduled arrival time in Morden is 3.15pm. The temperature in Morden is approximately 15 degrees celsius, and Morden is in the same time zone as Mill Hill east, so there is no need to adjust your watches.'

Piccadilly Line: 'Please allow the doors to close. Try not to confuse this with "Please hold the doors open." The two are distinct and separate instructions.'

Jubilee Line (while stuck in a tunnel): 'Well, ladies and gentlemen, I'm pleased to tell you it's a lovely sunny day outside. But of course you wouldn't know that, because you're sitting in the dark.'

Piccadilly Line: 'To the gentleman wearing the long grey coat trying to get on the second carriage, what part of "Stand clear of the doors" don't you understand?'

Waterloo and City: 'Well ladies and gentlemen. I can see a light in front of me which I think is probably Bank Station, so that's good isn't it? But I personally was hoping for Calais. Perhaps next time, eh?'

District Line: 'May I remind all passengers that there is strictly no smoking allowed on any part of the Underground. However, if you are smoking a joint, it is only fair that you pass it round the rest of the carriage.'

Central Line: 'Ladies and gentlemen, I do apologise for the delay to your service. I know you're all dying to get home, unless, of course, you happen to be married to my ex-wife, in which case you'll want to cross over to the Westbound and go in the opposite direction.'

Central Line: 'Next time, you might find it easier to wait until the doors are open before trying to get on the train.'

At Barking: 'We're sorry for the delay. This is because the train is waiting for a new driver. Not that there was anything wrong with the old one. But we're waiting for a new one.'

Northern Line: 'Ladies and gentlemen, this train has 22 doors on each side, please feel free to use all of them, not just the two in the middle.'

Piccadilly Line: 'The next stop is Arsenal. For those of you that wish to see Tony Adams standing around for 90 minutes with his arm in the air, please get off here.'

Northern Line: 'Ladies and gentlemen we will shortly be arriving at Waterloo, then I think we will carry right on through the Channel Tunnel and spend the weekend in Paris.'

On the DLR to Bank (just after the line had opened): 'We are now approaching the new tunnel, so, after three... one, two, three, wheeeeeeeeeeeeeeeeeeeee!'

Victoria Line: 'This is Green Park, ladies and gentlemen, welcome to Grrreeeen Park. Change here for the Jubilee Line if you're desperate. Hope you've got plenty of time if you go for that one.'

Central Line: 'Apologies for the delay but we have lost power to the train as you can tell by the blinding speed at which we're travelling.'

District Line: 'To the hilarious gentleman who just showed me his bum, can I suggest that you join a gym or go on a diet.'

At Aldgate East station: 'Please use all available doors, there are some really good ones at the front of the train.'

Piccadilly Line: 'Please mind the gap when leaving the train. If you're not leaving the train, there's no need to mind the gap. It's all right, you're safe.'

In the Mornington Crescent elevator: 'This is Big Brother, there will be no voting in this room, please wait until you arrive at the diary room.'

District Line: 'All stations to Upminster with the exception of Cannon Street, this does not stop there on Saturdays due to total lack of interest.'

Jubilee Line: 'I'm not an axe-murdering, baby-eating lunatic who's going to drive this train off a precipice, you know. A smile would be nice.'

Bakerloo Line: 'When the gentleman on platform four has finished his phone conversation, would he kindly tell us how he gets mobile phone service down here when the rest of us can't? Thank you.'

District Line: 'Welcome aboard the Flintstones railway. Once I get my feet on the floor and start running we should be on our way.'

Waterloo and City Line: 'Good evening ladies and gents, and welcome to the Waterloo and City line. Sights to observe on the journey are, to your right, black walls and, to your left, black walls. See the lovely black walls as we make our way to Waterloo. We will shortly be arriving at Waterloo where this train will terminate. We would like to offer you a glass of champagne on arrival and you will notice the platform will be lined with lap-dancers for your entertainment. Have a good weekend.'

Northern Line: 'This train is going to Edgware. Eventually.'

With grateful thanks to
www.going-underground.net

Depth, in metres, of London Underground's deepest lift shaft, at Hampstead 55

SIGNIFICANT STATUES

Cleopatra's Needle

Cleopatra's Needle is an unlikely piece of history to find on the banks of a river in an English city. The obelisk, made of pink granite that was quarried in Syene, is one of a pair that once stood in front of the temple of Heliopolis, where Moses was born. Erected in Egypt around 1500 BC, the hieroglyphics in its surface were carved in praise of Pharaoh Thothmes III, and later of Rameses the Great. It was moved to Alexandria, Cleopatra's royal city, after her death, in 12 BC.

The obelisk was offered by the Viceroy of Egypt to the British people in 1819 as 'a worthy memorial of our distinguished countrymen Nelson and Abercromby', after Nelson's victory over the French in the Battle of the Nile in 1798. However, it was left to languish in the Alexandrian sands for 70 years before General Sir James Alexander arranged to have it transported to England. Encased in an iron cylinder, it was abandoned during a storm at the Bay of Biscay, but later recovered and brought to London. The plaques mounted around the base tell this story, and commemorate the men who died in the transportation of the stone. The bronze lions that flank it are more Victorian than Egyptian, but provide a suitably grand setting. In 1917 it gained the unfortunate distinction of being the first London monument to be hit in an air attack during World War One; a bomb exploded nearby and the plinth and the right-hand lion suffered shrapnel damage, which is still visible in a series of pockmarks in the stone and bronze.

But the 180-tonne, 68.5-foot monolith holds a further historical secret; its plinth contains historical items such as a full set of British Empire coins, Imperial weights and measures, Bibles in various languages, a railway guide and copies of newspapers from 1879, the year in which it was erected on the Embankment.

LONDON WORDS

7 September 1666

Up by 5-a-clock and, blessed be God, find all well, and by water to Paul's wharfe. Walked thence and saw all the town burned, and a miserable sight of Pauls church, with all the roofs fallen and the body of the Quire fallen into St Fayths – Pauls school also – Ludgate – Fleet street – my father's house, and the church, and a good part of the Temple the like. So to Creeds lodging near the New Exchange, and there find him laid down upon a bed – the house all unfurnished, there being fears of the fire's coming to them.

Samuel Pepys, *Diary*

RIOTING IN THE STREETS

In 1870, MP Lord George Gordon, President of the Protestant Association, incited a huge and angry crowd to protest against the dilution of anti-Catholic laws, which until that point had prevented Catholics from owning property, inheriting land and other essential functions. Amid rumours that tens of thousands of Jesuits were concealed in tunnels underneath London, ready to storm the city at any moment, a mob of around 30,000 – some accounts place the total at nearer 50,000 – began rioting on Friday 2 June 1870 with attacks on Catholic places of worship, including the Sardinian Chapel in WC1 and the Bavarian Chapel on Warwick Street. The riots flared over the weekend and continued on until the Tuesday, when Newgate and Clink prisons were attacked and set on fire. The rioters attacked Catholic churches and buildings, judges and other dignitaries, and a group of French protestants (by mistake). The riots were said to be the most violent in London's history. They attacked the Bank of England and threatened the Mint and the Royal Arsenal, as well as breaking into a distillery, which they also set on fire. Twenty rioters were overwhelmed by the quantities of free drink suddenly available to them, and drank themselves to death. Eventually the militia was called in to restore order, 285 rioters were killed and 450 more imprisoned. Twenty-five were later hanged, although the original troublemaker, Lord Gordon, surrendered and was cleared of treason. He was later sent to Newgate Prison, once it had been rebuilt, for libelling Marie Antoinette, and he died within its walls.

SOHO SHELTER

The charming little mock-Tudor hut at the centre of Soho Square looks like a very upmarket gardener's shed. It in fact once housed a transformer for the Charing Cross Electric Light Company, and stands over one of the many abandoned underground shelters that were built during World War Two.

QUOTE UNQUOTE

It is not the walls that make the city, but the people who live within them. The walls of London may be battered, but the spirit of the Londoner stands resolute and undismayed.
King George VI, in a broadcast on 23 September 1940, to the Empire during German bomber offensive.

THE DAY THE MUSIC DIED

Nine musicians who met their end in London

Marc Bolan
16 September 1977
The lead singer with T-Rex crashed into a tree on Barnes Common, where tributes are still left by grieving fans.

Graham Bond
8 May 1974
The founder member of the Graham Bond Organisation fell under a tube train at Finsbury Park.

Sandy Denny
21 April 1978
Fairport Convention's former lead singer died of a cerebral haemorrhage after falling down a flight of stairs a month earlier.

Jimmy McCulloch
27 September 1979
The guitarist with Wings was found dead in his London flat, allegedly of a drug-related heart failure.

Jimi Hendrix
18 September 1970
Probably the greatest guitarist in history died on arrival at St Mary Abbots Hospital after choking on his own vomit as the result of a barbiturates overdose.

'Mama' Cass Elliot
29 July 1974
The generously sized singer from the Mamas and Papas died of a heart attack.

Pete Farndon
14 April 1983
The Pretenders' bass guitarist died of a drug overdose.

Keith Moon
7 September 1978
The drummer with The Who died in his sleep after an overdose of anti-seizure medication, rather than of the recreational drugs that were first suspected.

QUOTE UNQUOTE

London is a modern Babylon.
Benjamin Disraeli, statesman and author

LONG TALL ALLEY

The narrowest alleyway in London is Brydges Place, which connects Bedfordbury in Covent Garden to St Martin's Lane. Two hundred yards long, it is, at its narrowest point, only 15 inches wide. It is also dark, dank and faintly odorous, and never sees the sunshine. For those of a mischievous mind, it is also a good place out of which to dart unexpectedly, in order to alarm innocent tourists.

The Bloomsbury Group was one of England's best-known artistic groups, although its members were known as much for their unconventional lifestyle as for their work. It was begun by Thoby Stephen, brother of Virginia Woolf, who began holding art discussion evenings at 46 Gordon Square after leaving university. The group flourished despite public disapproval of its somewhat incestuous relationships.

Key members:
Clive Bell, art critic and husband of Vanessa Stephen
Gwen Darwin, granddaughter of Charles Darwin
EM Forster, novelist
Roger Fry, critic
John Maynard Keynes, economist
Vanessa Stephen, staged Britain's first exhibition of Post-Impressionist paintings with Bell
Lytton Strachey, biographer, lover of artist Dora Carrington and of Ralph Partridge, Dora's husband
Lytton Strachey's sister, Marjorie
Virginia Woolf, novelist and lover of Vita Sackville-West, and biographer of Roger Fry

Satirised in: *The Apes of God* by Wyndham Lewis (1930)

Criticised by: DH Lawrence, who called them 'this horror of little swarming selves' and Wyndham Lewis, who referred to them as 'elitist, corrupt and talentless'.

Famous addresses:
37 Gordon Square: Vanessa Bell and Duncan Grant lived here in 1925.
46 Gordon Square: Virginia Woolf lived here from 1904–07, with her sister Vanessa and their brothers Adrian and Thoby. It became the main meeting place for the Bloomsbury Group. After Thoby Stephen's death, Clive and Vanessa Bell moved in. John Maynard Keynes also lived here.
50 Gordon Square: Clive Bell lived here from 1922–39; another Bloomsbury Group meeting place.
51 Gordon Square: Lytton Strachey lived here 1919–24, and wrote his biography of Queen Victoria (1921) here.
38 Brunswick Square: Virginia Woolf and John Maynard Keynes lived here in 1911–12
34 Mecklenburgh Square: Virginia Woolf worked here before World War One and included the building in *Night and Day*. Also the home of the Women's Trade Union League.
37 Mecklenburgh Square: Virginia and Leonard Woolf lived here from 1939–40, and Virginia finished her biography of Roger Fry here. The house was damaged in the Blitz and no longer stands.
52 Tavistock Square: Virginia Woolf lived here with her husband, Leonard from 1924–39. The couple ran their publishing company, Hogarth Press, from these premises and Virginia wrote most of her novels here. The house was destroyed in the Blitz, and is now the site of the Tavistock Hotel.

The original meanings of a few London place names

Acton ....*farmstead by the oaks*
Barnet ....*land cleared by burning*
Clerkenwell ....*spring where students gather*
Dulwich..*marshy meadow where dill grows*
Ealing ....*settlement of Gilla's people*
Fulham .... *Fulla's land in a river bend*
Greenwich ....*green harbour*
Hammersmith ....*place with a hammer smithy*
Islington... *Gisla's hill*
Kensal Green ....*place by the king's wood*
Lambeth..*landing place for lambs*
Mayfair...*the place of the May fair*
                       (held there in seventeenth and eighteenth century)
Neasden...*place by the nose-shaped hill*
Osterley ....*woodland clearing with a sheepfold*
Putney.......................................*landing place where hawks are seen*
Roehampton...................................*home farm where rooks are seen*
Spitalfields ....*hospital fields*
Theydon Bois ....*de Bosco's estate in the valley*
                          where thatching materials are obtained
Upminster ....*higher church*
Vauxhall..*Falke's hall or manor*
Walthamstow ....*place where guests are welcome*

CAPITAL CONUNDRUMS

Who was the first person to have a blue plaque attached to the
house where they had lived?
Answer on page 153.

LONDON WORDS

It is recorded that late one night in Trafalgar Square an old gentleman, slightly the worse for drink, was observed apparently searching for something on the pavement. A constable approached and
said: 'What's the matter, sir? Have you lost something?'

'Yes,' said the old gentleman, feebly. 'I've lost my purse.'

It seemed rather an odd place to lose a purse and the constable
said: 'Are you sure you lost it hereabouts?'

'Oh no,' replied the old gent, 'I lost it in Dover Street, but
Trafalgar Square is so much better lighted.'

HM Howgrave-Graham, *Light and Shade at Scotland Yard*

Back in the late 19th century, the Regent's Park Slow Motion Players had great success with their version of The Matrix.

LONDON BRIDGE IS LEAVING TOWN

In the 1960s the heavy traffic in London meant that the old London Bridge was falling down. Meetings were held by the London council to decide what to do with the bridge, and it was the suggestion of a man named Ivan Luckin that it should be sold to the Americans. As well as being a London councillor, Luckin owned an advertising company and travelled to America regularly on business. He told the council that he believed the Americans would be keen to buy the bridge, and to own a piece of English history. His idea was ridiculed, but Luckin was adamant, and visited America with the Town Clerk of London to promote the sale. Four hundred television stations, radio stations and newspapers attended the press conference and the bridge was duly sold in 1968 for $2,460,000 to Robert McCulloch of McCulloch Oil, who had the bridge disassembled, transported and rebuilt in Arizona, where it has become a major tourist attraction. While disdainful Brits like to joke that the oil baron thought he was getting Tower Bridge, Ivan Luckin strongly disputes this rumour. The bridge was further immortalised in the *Guinness Book of Records* as the largest antique in the world to be sold.

Eros

Eros, the monument that lends a little romance to the neon-lit surroundings of Piccadilly Circus, is not in fact Eros, the God of Love, but is instead the Angel of Christian Charity. And it's not a statue, but a memorial fountain. Erected in 1893 in memory of Victorian philanthropist Lord Shaftesbury, it has become a resting place and photo-opportunity for tired tourists and courting couples. It was given the name of Statue of Eros within days of its unveiling in June 1893, not least because the sculptor, Sir Arthur Gilbert, said that his work represented 'the blindfolded love sending forth his missile of kindness'. He meant Christian love, but the naked, Cupid-like figure seems to represent the more earthly kind of affections. The figure itself used to be golden, but the original has been replaced by a lead copy. The angel shooting an arrow is supposed to be a pun on Shaftesbury – the angel is aiming downwards to 'bury' the 'shaft' of the arrow in the ground

The memorial itself nearly ruined its sculptor; Gilbert originally planned it as a drinking fountain and wanted to make it bigger to make it easier to drink from. But the London County Council disagreed, even though that is exactly what the critics picked on when it was opened (and they blamed Gilbert). Had he had his way, it would be a much more impressive object, with the angel floating apparently unsupported above a gushing fountain. As it was, Gilbert claimed that it traumatised the rest of his life.

NOT THAT LONDON

London is the capital of Christmas Island in Polynesia. 'Discovered' on Christmas Day 1643, the island was purchased from the Singapore government by Australia for £2.9 million pounds in 1957 and is now an Australian territory. Population: 433

London is also an industrial city in south-east Ontario, Canada, which bears some parallels to its English namesake. It has its own Victoria Park, Covent Garden Market, St Paul's Cathedral, Blackfriars Bridge and district of Ealing, and the centre was destroyed by fire in 1844 and 1845 and rebuilt. Population: 336,539.

QUOTE UNQUOTE

London landladies are Britannias armed with helmet, shield, trident, and have faces with the word 'No' stamped like a coat of arms on them.
VS Pritchett, writer

Year in 1900s when London was covered for three days by a fog so bad that residents were advised to breathe through makeshift masks

CHURCH ROADS

For centuries, churches were built along ley lines, and people continued to use the ley line as a thoroughfare, walking straight through the centre of the church on their way to somewhere else. This was the case with St Paul's cathedral, when it was common practice for people taking their goods to market to walk right down the aisle and through the cloisters, even during services, complete with their cattle and horses.

GET BACK IN YOUR BOX

Items thrown at illusionist David Blaine when he spent 44 days without food in a perspex box over the Thames in 2003
Eggs
Golf balls
Balloons filled with pink paint
Bananas
Bottles
Chips

Things he threw back (as souvenirs for his fans)
Pencils
Socks
Toilet roll
A strip of black bin liner

Other distracting events
His water supply pipe was cut
Women flashed their breasts at him
He was mooned
People banged drums to keep him awake
Laser pens were shone into the box
A remote control helicopter carrying a
beefburger was flown up to the box

LONDON WORDS

It might have been Fortanon. It could have been Fortyahan. It hovered for years between Fortnam and Fortnane. It wasn't until 1707 that it settled down into Fortnum, collected its Mason and became the sweetest sound in the English language for those countless perceptive thousands who know that life can be sustained by bread and water but is given a sharp, upward boost by the more imaginative combination of caviar and champagne.

From *The Delectable History of Fortnum & Mason*,
a booklet distributed to patrons

In 1348 the Great Plague that had been devastating Europe finally reached Britain. It was probably not, as was widely believed, bubonic plague, and was not referred to at the time as the Black Death, a phrase that was invented later to differentiate between the plague of 1348–1350 and the later Great Plague of London that began in 1665. But it still cut a terrifying swathe through London.

The worst of the deaths were concentrated into three or four months, but in the overcrowded, unsanitary city, the disease continued to flourish until well into 1350. In early 1349, around 200 bodies a day were being buried in hastily dug plague pits. The Plague took rich and poor alike; the rich tried to flee the city, but only took the disease with them. Even the Archbishop of Canterbury was not immune; John Offord died in May 1349 before he had been enthroned, and his successor died in August. It is estimated that around 20,000 Londoners were killed by the Plague, around a third of the population. What was worse was that plague would return to London at regular intervals for centuries to come.

The Great Plague of 1665 was the worst outbreak of this feared disease, and London was hit hardest. The hot summer of 1665 together with the city's increasingly over-crowded population created ideal conditions for the spread of an infectious disease. While the wealthy fled to the country – again taking the disease with them – the poor were not allowed to leave the filthy slums. Some who could not escape even took to living on boats on the Thames to try to isolate themselves.

Some measures were taken to contain the disease. Dogs and cats were killed as they were thought to be the transmitters. If a person fell ill, the whole family would be locked into their house for 40 days. A red cross on the door signalled that a house was sealed. Plague doctors and nurses were not qualified in any way and usually did little more than sell food to the quarantined families. 'Searchers' were paid to collect bodies and would roam the streets, calling: 'Bring out your dead!' The death toll was breathtaking: thousands died every week, reaching a peak of 7,165 in one week in September. Bodies were buried in mass graves and new plague pits were dug in Aldgate, Blackheath and Finsbury Fields. Though it is impossible to calculate an exact death toll, historians now believe that around 100,000 people died in London during this last Great Plague.

In view of this, The Great Fire of 1666 was almost a blessing – it killed only six people, but destroyed large parts of London and practically all its slums, which at last led to the end of the plague epidemic.

Distance, in millions of kilometres, travelled in total by all Tube trains in an average year

Did you know...?

The Castle, Cowcross Street EC1
The only pub in England to have a pawnbroker's license.

Hand and Shears, Middle Street, Cloth Fair EC1
Prisoners had their cases heard upstairs and if the judgment went against them, they were allowed a drink at the bar on their way to the gallows.

Hoop and Grapes, 47 Aldgate High Street EC3
Thirteenth century inn, the oldest non-ecclesiastical building in the City.

Ship Tavern, Lime Street EC3
Built in 1447.

Ship and Blue Ball, Boundary Road E2
The Great Train Robbery was planned here in the Sixties, and, allegedly, a false wall in the games room concealed the stolen millions.

Old Nun's Head, Nunhead Green SE15
The inn stands on the site of a nunnery which was demolished in the Reformation. The abbess was decapitated, and her head displayed on a pole.

Ladbroke Arms, Ladbroke Road W12
The pub was won by Lord Ladbroke in payment of a gambling debt.

The Dove, Upper Mall W6
Rule Britannia was written here; Nell Gwynne, Ernest Hemingway and Graham Greene drank here; it has the smallest recorded bar: 4ft 2in by 7ft 10in.

Town of Ramsgate, Wapping High Street E1
Colonel Blood was captured here as he tried to steal the Crown Jewels; the hanging judge, Judge Jeffries, was also captured here.

THE 21 TOWERS OF LONDON

The Tower of London is made up of 21 towers, 20 of which are still standing:

Beauchamp • Bell • Bloody
Bowyer • Brick • Broad Arrow
Byward • Constable • Cradle
Devereux • Develin • Flint
Lanthorn • Martin • Middle
Salt • St Thomas's • Wakefield
Wardrobe (no longer standing)
Well • White (the oldest)

When the station we now know as Embankment was opened in May 1870, serving the District Line, it was given the name of Charing Cross. When the Bakerloo line platforms opened there on 10 March 1906, the station was renamed Embankment.

Meanwhile, the station now known as Charing Cross – which also opened to serve the Bakerloo line on 10 March 1906 – was called Trafalgar Square, but was renamed Charing Cross when the Northern Line platforms opened there in June 1907. When the Northern Line platforms also opened at Embankment on 6 April 1914, that station's name was changed again to Charing Cross (Embankment). On the same day, Charing Cross station became Charing Cross (Strand). A year later, on 9 May 1915, both names changed again: Charing Cross (Strand) became Strand and Charing Cross (Embankment) was renamed Charing Cross.

Strand was closed for rebuilding in June 1973; while it was closed, Embankment was renamed Charing Cross Embankment. When Strand reopened on 1 May 1979, now serving the Bakerloo, Northern and Jubilee lines, it was renamed Charing Cross. And finally, on 12 September 1976, Charing Cross Embankment was renamed, simply, Embankment.

And that, we hope, is the end of that.

LONDON WORDS

I have passed all my days in London, until I have formed as many and intense local attachments as any of you mountaineers can have done with dead nature. The lighted shops of the Strand and Fleet Street, the innumerable trades, tradesmen, and customers, coaches, waggons, playhouses, all the bustle and wickedness round about Covent Garden, the very women of the town, the watchmen, drunken scenes, rattles,—life awake, if you awake, at all hours of the night, the impossibility of being dull in Fleet Street, the crowds, the very dirt and mud, the sun shining upon houses and pavements, the print shops, the old book stalls, parsons cheap'ning books, coffee houses, steam of soups from kitchens, pantomimes, London itself a pantomime and a masquerade,—all these things work themselves into my mind and feed me, without a power of satiating me. The wonder of these sights impells me into night-walks about her crowded streets, I often shed tears in the Strand from fullness of joy at so much life.

Charles Lamb, *British essayist and critic*
in a letter to William Wordsworth, 30 January 1801

WHEN THE THAMES FREEZES OVER

When severe winter weather hit London in centuries past, it was possible for the Thames to freeze so hard that the city's traders could hold a fair on the ice. But the Frost Fairs, as they were called, came about only because of London Bridge. When the 'new' stone bridge was first built in 1176, replacing the old wooden version, its 19 narrow arches slowed the flow of water down so much that the river was able to freeze when temperatures dropped. Although the residents ventured on to the frozen river many times, the first real Frost Fair was not held until 1564, when stalls, sideshows and many forms of entertainment, including merry-go-rounds and donkey races were set up on the ice, which remained frozen for two months. The river froze many times after that, although the Frost Fairs took place only four more times, in 1684, 1716, 1740 and 1814. The last began on 1 February, and stretched from Blackfriars to Three Crane Stairs. A 'road' took shape across the river from bank to bank and was temporarily named City Road. Stalls, sideshows and other entertainments were set up, and even a printing press or two was installed to print souvenirs of the great fair. The ice was not entirely safe; one or two people who strayed from the centre of activities fell through cracks in the ice, and a large piece of ice broke off near London Bridge, carrying away a man and two boys. Fortunately they lay on the ice, and were soon rescued by some Billingsgate fishermen. Apart from this, the fair passed without incident, lasting a full week until rain set in and the ice began to thaw. It was gone in a few days; and when the old London Bridge was replaced in 1831, its new design no longer slowed down the river's flow, and that was the end of the Frost Fairs.

SPORTING LONDON

In London in July 1985, Boris Becker became the youngest man ever to win Wimbledon, when at the age of 17 years and 7 months he beat the unseeded Kevin Curran in four sets: 6-3, 6-7, 7-6, 6-4. He broke two more records that day; he was also the first German and the first unseeded player to win the tournament. To dismiss claims of a fluke, he beat Ivan Lendl the following year to take the title again, and reached the finals in the following three years, winning for the third and last time in 1989 by beating Stefan Edberg in three sets. Edberg got his own back the following year, when the pair faced each other in the finals once more, and Edberg beat Becker in five gruelling sets. In all, Becker reached the Wimbledon finals seven times in 10 years.

The early fires of London

Around the year 130, fire swept through London, destroying 100 acres from Newgate Street in the west to the area around the Tower of London. As most buildings were made of wattle-and-daub and timber, the effects were predictably devastating. Some areas such as Southwark were abandoned completely and remained so for many years.

In the seventh century, St Paul's Cathedral, then made of wood, burned down. At the time many houses were built with protruding upper storeys that almost met across the road below, creating a wind tunnel that exacerbated any fire that broke out.

To reduce the risk of fire, William the Conqueror introduced the *couvre feu*, or curfew, which meant that all fires and lights had to be extinguished at 8 o'clock every night. But in 1077 there was another huge fire in the city, and in 1087 yet another, which again burned down St Paul's and a large chunk of London.

Further fires came in 1093, 1132 and 1135, the last of which burned down London Bridge. The city's wooden buildings and lack of firefighting equipment – and the belief that a serious fire was an act of God and could be stopped only by prayer – did not help the situation, and fire was a constant hazard. The first mayor of London, Henry Fitzailwyn, tried to improve matters by insisting that buildings be made

of stone and without thatched roofs, but he made little impression.

The first Great Fire of London was in 1212, which broke out on 11 July in Southwark. Crowds of people surged on to London Bridge to watch, but the fire spread so rapidly that many were trapped on the burning bridge, and few survived the leap into the river below. It is not known how many people died, although some reports suggest that it was around 3,000.

Four further major fires followed, and in 1497 Henry VII had to flee Sheen Palace in Richmond, which was destroyed by fire. As London grew and more houses were built, proper chimneys were installed, although some were made of hollowed tree trunks, which didn't help matters. Also many tradesmen who used fires for their work were operating in cramped conditions in residential areas.

By 1600 the first fire engines were in use, although they were hand-pumped and useful only for small fires. King James I tried to encourage the use of stone in building, but only a few years after his death, in 1633, a large fire swept across London Bridge and along the riverbank, setting the wooden houses alight as it went. Fifty or more houses were destroyed and several people killed. But these were mere practice runs compared to the terrible fire that was to come.

OLD PICTURE, NEW CAPTION

*Arthur spent his Sundays thinking up new ways to avoid
the congestion charge*

CAPITAL CONUNDRUMS

Which two London Underground stations have
all five vowels in their names?
Answer on page 153.

MIND THE GAP, DEAR

When London architect Mike Kelly left the City for a new home in
Herefordshire, he missed his favourite Tube trains so much – in which
he had ridden since he was a child – that he took one of them with
him. When he heard that the 1959 rolling stock on the Northern Line
was to be replaced, he tracked down his favourite car, no 1304, and
rescued it from a North London siding. He installed it in his back
garden on a bit of track and it now provides an interesting venue for
afternoon tea when the weather's nice.

The tug was worked by two men, and with much toil went comparatively slowly. The clear moon that had lit up Chiswick had gone down by the time that they passed Battersea, and when they came under the enormous bulk of Westminster, day had already begun to break. It broke like the splitting of great bars of lead, showing bars of silver; and these had brightened like white fire when the tug, changing its onward course, turned inward to a large landing stage rather beyond Charing Cross.

The great stones of the Embankment seemed equally dark and gigantic as Syme looked up at them. They were big and black against the huge white dawn. They made him feel that he was landing on the colossal steps of some Egyptian palace; and, indeed, the thing suited his mood, for he was, in his own mind, mounting to attack the solid thrones of horrible and heathen kings. He leapt out of the boat on to one slimy step, and stood, a dark and slender figure, amid the enormous masonry. The two men in the tug put her off again and turned up stream. They had never spoken a word.

GK Chesterton, *The Man Who Was Thursday*

QUOTE UNQUOTE

The young men of the age lose five, ten, fifteen thousand pounds in an evening there. Lord Stavordale, not one and twenty, lost £11,000 there last Tuesday but recovered it by one great hand at hazard: he swore a great oath – 'Now if I had been playing deep, I might have won millions!'
Horace Walpole, eighteenth century politician, complaining in 1770 about the reckless gambling that was rife among the upper classes

HERE TODAY, GONE TOMORROW

The *London Daily News* had possibly the shortest career of any UK newspaper. Launched on 24 February 1987 by the ebullient Robert Maxwell, it closed on 23 July the same year. Maxwell, who was by then owner of the Mirror Group, wanted his new rag to be the first 24-hour newspaper in Britain and cheaper than all its rivals. But Associated Newspapers, publishers of the *Daily News*'s competitor, the *Evening Standard*, fought back and undermined Maxwell's attempt by relaunching the defunct *Evening News* at an even lower price, at which Maxwell was forced to admit defeat. It is estimated that the exercise cost him around £50 million.

Percentage of Britain's theatre box office revenues that are earned by London theatres

TUBE MANNERS

Ten things to avoid doing on the Tube, as seen by regular passengers

- Singing to your CD player (we can hear you)
- Nodding your head vigorously in time to the music (we can see you)
- Thinking that because you are wearing headphones this also makes you invisible and starting to pick your nose (we can still see you)
- Watching porn on your laptop, which you downloaded last night (we can see you, and we'd really rather not)
- Glaring at passengers every time they shift slightly in their seat, because you think it means they are getting off at the next stop, and you want to sit down
- French kissing
- Talking to someone who doesn't want to talk to you
- Having a pee at the end of the carriage (because, obviously, that's better than doing it in the middle of the carriage)
- Sitting on the outside seat and then looking irritated when someone squeezes past you to get to the empty window seat
- Throwing up without warning. Or even with warning.

YOUR NAME IN LIGHTS

The neon advertisements of Piccadilly Circus took root before neon was invented, when a set of buildings was demolished at the end of Glasshouse Street in 1886. It was intended to improve access to the newly constructed Shaftesbury Avenue, but it gave property owners whose buildings now faced directly on to the Circus an idea. Making good use of the newly invented electric advertisements, they put illuminated signs on the roofs of their buildings. The London County Council objected on the grounds of vulgarity and managed to get them taken down. But the building owners simply reattached the signs to the front of their buildings instead. The law as it stood did not prevent this, as most of the building leases had been drawn up before the invention of such illuminations and weren't precise enough to outlaw the ads. The council found that it could order their removal only if they were a threat to pedestrian safety, but when they tried to do so, the courts judged that the signs were safe, and there they have remained ever since. However, many buildings around the Circus are Crown Estate properties, whose leases were better able to prevent the attachment of any such signs to their buildings – which is why the neon boards are concentrated in one or two places rather than filling the whole circus.

The swans on the Thames are jointly owned by the reigning monarch and two of the City Livery Companies, the Vintners and the Dyers, a privilege that has existed for 600 years. The swans have always been protected by draconian laws: in the mid-nineteenth century one could be transported for seven years for harming a swan; by the end of the century the penalty was less alarming, although it would still earn the culprit seven weeks' hard labour. Once a year in July, the rightful owners gather at the side of the Thames to count, mark and pinion (clip the wings) the season's new cygnets. The Dyers' swans are marked with one notch to the upper beak, the Vintners' swans have two notches. The Queen's swans are unmarked.

Swan upping probably refers to the fact that the swans have to be taken out of the water to be marked. The ceremony is conducted by three Swan Herdsmen and their teams of Swan Uppers, who set out to row from Temple Stairs to Henley, their boats decorated with their Livery banners. As the boats approach Windsor Castle, the occupants stand (carefully) to attention and salute 'Her Majesty the Queen, Seigneur of the Swans'. Also, the newest member of the team, known as the colt, is ducked in the river at some point in the proceedings.

LONDON MARATHON FACTS

- The first London marathon took place on 29 March 1982
- It was founded by former Olympic champion Chris Brasher
- The first sponsor was Gillette, who stumped up £50,000
- In 1982, 20,000 people applied to enter the marathon. This rose to 80,500 in 2004
- In 1982, 7,747 were accepted; this was 46,500 in 2004
- 6,255 runners crossed the finish line in 1982, compared to 32,563 in 2004
- Other sponsors have included Mars (1983–88), Nutrasweet (1993–95), Flora (1996–2006)
- In 2004, identical quadruplets Alison, Brooke, Claire and Darcy Hansen all ran the marathon, at the risk of making the other competitors think they were seeing things
- Favourite costumes: two men wearing a strap-on plastic Mini Cooper body (2001); a man dressed up as a phone box (2004)
- One of the slowest ever finishing times was set in 2003 by a man in a vintage 130lb diving suit, who took five days, eight hours, 29 minutes and 46 seconds to finish the race
- The London Marathon has raised around £200 million for charity since 1982 and has become a world-renowned race

CANARY WHARF FACTS

Facts and figures about 1 Canada Square, better known as the Canary Wharf Tower

- It is 244 metres high, the tallest building in Britain.
- It has 50 floors.
- 90,000 square feet of Italian and Guatemalan marble were used in the lobby.
- It has 3,960 windows.
- There are 4,388 steps.
- It has 32 passenger lifts divided into four banks, each serving a different section of the building.
- It also has two freight lifts and two firemen's lifts.
- It takes 40 seconds for the lift to ascend from the lobby to the 50th floor.
- 27,500 metric tonnes of British Steel and 500,000 bolts were used in the construction of the tower.
- The exterior walls are clad by 370,000 square feet of stainless steel.
- The aircraft warning light at the very top of the tower flashes 40 times a minute, 57,600 times a day.
- Over 80,000 deliveries are made to the loading bay of the tower every year.

A HEARTFELT TALE

Bleeding Heart Yard was named by someone with a taste for the literal, as it was there that a seventeenth century society beauty was found dead after jilting her lover, the Spanish Ambassador. Elizabeth Hatton rejected her suitor in 1626, but was seen dancing with him at a ball not long afterwards. When she left the party, the other guests assumed she was with the Ambassador, but in fact she had been horribly murdered and her body was found outside in the yard the next morning. The case is referred to in Dickens's *Little Dorrit*: 'At dawn the body of Lady Hatton was found in the courtyard behind the stables torn limb from limb with her heart still pumping blood on to the cobblestones.' The site is now occupied by The Bleeding Heart Restaurant, which serves a fine rare steak.

QUOTE UNQUOTE

The London zoo is an animal microcosm of London, and even the lions, as a rule, behave as if they had been born in South Kensington.
Leonard Woolf, political theorist,
publisher and husband of Virginia Woolf

QUOTE UNQUOTE

The best bribe which London offers to-day to the imagination, is, that, in such a vast variety of people and conditions, one can believe there is room for persons of romantic character to exist, and that the poet, the mystic, and the hero may hope to confront their counterparts.

Ralph Waldo Emerson, essayist, poet and philosopher

WRITING ON THE WALL

Graffiti spotted in London

The grave of Karl Marx is just another communist plot
Charing Cross Road

Colin Davis can't tell his brass from his oboe
Royal Festival Hall

Lateral thinking is a con. Honest? Yes, straight up
London School of Economics

Good morning, lemmings
Facing commuters on the M4 as they enter London

God is not dead but alive and well and working on a much less ambitious project
On the wall of a Greenwich pub

THE CULTURAL COALMAN

Cultural life in London in the early 1700s was much encouraged by a humble coalman called Thomas Britton. Arriving in London in 1677, he established a coal business in Clerkenwell Green, living over 'the shop', and it was in his simple rooms that he held musical evenings every week for 40 years. The concerts attracted the likes of Handel as well as society leaders and dignitaries, who enjoyed a very high standard of entertainment, including a few turns by Handel on the five-stop organ. Britton also collected rare books and was helped in his business by the Earls of Oxford and Winchelsea, who would take their finds to a bookshop in Paternoster Row, where Britton would meet them after he had finished shifting his bags of coal. Britton's expertise and interest was such that he helped to form the Harleian Library, which became part of the British Library. Sadly after such a cultural life, he was killed by a practical joke in which a ventriloquist pretended to be the voice of God and warned Britton that he would die unless he immediately recited the Lord's Prayer. The superstitious coal merchant was taken ill and died a few days later. His portrait hangs in the National Gallery – in which he is dressed as a coalman

LONDON ON LOCATION

London has often pretended to be somewhere else...

Film: *Death Wish III*
Supposed to be: The Bronx, New York
Is actually: Lambeth Hospital

Film: *Empire of the Sun*
Supposed to be: Japanese internment camp
Is actually: Beckton Gas Works, Docklands

Film: *Eyes Wide Shut*
Supposed to be: Greenwich Village
Is actually: Berners Street and Eastcastle Street

Film: *Eyes Wide Shut*
Supposed to be: Sonata, New York jazz club
Is actually: Madame Jo-Jo's, Soho

Film: *Full Metal Jacket*
Supposed to be: Vietnam
Is actually: Beckton Gas Works, Docklands

Film: *The Hunger*
Supposed to be: New York clinic
Is actually: Senate House, University College

Film: *Indiana Jones and the Last Crusade*
Supposed to be: Berlin airport
Is actually: Royal Horticultural Hall, Westminster

Film: *Mission: Impossible*
Supposed to be: CIA Headquarters
Is actually: County Hall, South Bank

Film: *Patriot Games*
Supposed to be: White House
Is actually: Royal Naval College, Greenwich

Film: *The Saint*
Supposed to be: American Embassy in Moscow
Is actually: Camden Town Hall

Film: *Shining Through*
Supposed to be: The Pentagon
Is actually: Royal Naval College, Greenwich

Film: *Spy Game*
Supposed to be: Virginia countryside
Is actually: Regent's Park

Films: *Superman IV, Patriot Games, An American Werewolf in London*
Supposed to be: New York underground
Is actually: Aldwych Underground station

Film: *Harry Potter and the Philosopher's Stone*
Supposed to be: Gringott's Wizarding Bank
Is actually: Australian High Commission

QUOTE UNQUOTE

London clubs remain insistent on keeping people out, long after they have stopped wanting to come in.
Anthony Sampson, writer

LONDON'S FESTIVALS, PARADES AND SHOWS

New Year's Day Parade, *January*
One way to beat the hangover: 10,000 performers from countries all over the world parade from Parliament Square to Piccadilly.

Chinese New Year, *January*
Chinatown plays host to tourists and residents alike, with music, dancing, fireworks and food stalls, from Soho to Trafalgar Square.

Oxford and Cambridge Boat Race, *March*
Seventeen minutes of frantic rowing for the teams; a whole day of drinking for the spectators.

Flora London Marathon, *April*
World-record holders compete with charity runners in fancy dress along 26 miles of London's streets.

Chelsea Flower Show, *May*
Garden design, plants and outdoor furniture and fierce competition in the heart of Chelsea.

Beating Retreat, *May*
Colourful military parade that began to mark the return of the troops to their barracks after combat, attended by the Queen and followed by a military band concert performed by the Massed Bands of the Household Division.

Royal Academy Summer Exhibition, *June*
Huge exhibition of amateur and semi-professional works of art.

Trooping the Colour, *June*
Celebration of the Queen's official birthday; stirring military parade dating back to early seventeenth century. Beginning at the Horse Guards Parade, it continues down the Mall, where it can be watched for free.

Hampton Court Palace Flower Show, *July*
Larger and less posh than Chelsea, a superb flower show in an equally superb setting.

BBC Henry Wood Promenade Concerts, *July-September*
Series of classical concerts at the Royal Albert Hall, famous for its noisy and rumbustious Last Night of the Proms.

Notting Hill Carnival, *August*
Loud and colourful, celebration of Afro-Caribbean culture, with floats, parades, food and DJs on every corner.

Thames Festival, *September*
The end of the Coin Street Festival, with illuminated procession and river events.

London Open House, *September*
An annual opportunity to go behind closed doors, and see inside some of London's most beautiful and historic buildings.

Lord Mayor's Show, *November*
Huge procession from Guildhall to Waterloo Bridge, led by the mayor in his State coach; ends with fireworks on the Thames.

76 *Amount, in thousands of tonnes, of soot that was falling on London every year by 1912*

BOOKS WITH LONDON TITLES

Liza of Lambeth, Somerset Maugham, *1897*
The Napoleon of Notting Hill, GK Chesterton, *1904*
Psmith in the City, PG Wodehouse, *1910*
Down and Out in Paris and London, George Orwell, *1933*
London Belongs To Me, Norman Collins, *1945*
The Ballad of Peckham Rye, Muriel Spark, *1960*
Black Hearts in Battersea, Joan Aiken, *1965*
The British Museum is Falling Down, David Lodge, *1965*
84 Charing Cross Road, Helene Hanff, *1970*
London Fields, Martin Amis, *1989*
A Year in Cricklewood, Alan Coren, *1991*
London: The Novel, Edward Rutherfurd, *1997*
Mother London, Michael Moorcock, *2000*
Camberwell Beauty, Jenny Éclair, *2001*
London Boulevard, Ken Bruen, *2001*
The Whitechapel Conspiracy, Ann Perry, *2001*
Only in London, Hanan Al-Shaykh, *2002*

OLDEST RESTAURANT

Rules is the oldest restaurant in London that is still in its original location, on Maiden Lane in Covent Garden. Established by Thomas Rule in 1798, it now serves traditional British food, specialising in game, oysters, pies and puddings. Rules was the favourite spot for Edward VII, when he was still Prince of Wales, for wining and dining his mistress, the actress Lillie Langtry. Their signed portraits still hang on the walls of the King Edward VII Room.

A LOAD OF BOLLARDS

London is full of bollards. Those erected in Georgian times were mostly, and enterprisingly, made from disused cannons, with a defunct cannonball blocking the mouth, in the reverse process to melting down iron railings to make weapons. Examples of these military structures can be seen in India Street in EC3 and at the end of Old Barge House Alley in Blackfriars. A large proportion of bollards date from just after the Battle of Waterloo, such as the ones marked Sommers Town in Pancras Road, and others marked Clink and either 1812 or 1825, which were made by the Clink Pavement Company. The bollards in the Strand are shaped like rockets, the Imperial War Museum, fittingly, has bollards shaped like shells and the bollards in Cavendish Court W1 have an almost phallic appearance.

OLD PICTURE, NEW CAPTION

*In its early days, the National Gallery experimented with
various ways to encourage visitors to linger longer*

LONDON WORDS

'I think Hurree Babu is getting too old for the Road. He likes better
to collect manners and customs information. Yes, he wants to be an
FRS.'

...No money and no preferment would have drawn Creighton
from his work on the Indian Survey, but deep in his heart also lay the
ambition to write 'FRS' after his name. Honours of a sort he knew
could be obtained by ingenuity and the help of friends, but, to the
best of his belief, nothing save work – papers representing a life of it
– took a man into the Society which he had bombarded for years
with monographs on strange Asiatic cults and unknown customs.
Nine men out of ten would flee from a Royal Society soirée in
extremity of boredom; but Creighton was the tenth, and at times his
soul yearned for the crowded rooms in easy London where silver-
haired, bald-headed gentlemen who know nothing of the Army move
among spectroscopic experiments, the lesser plants of the frozen
tundras, electric flight-measuring machines, and apparatus for slicing
into fractional millimetres the left eye of the female mosquito. By all
right and reason, it was the Royal Geographical that should have
appealed to him, but men are as chancy as children in their choice of
playthings. So Creighton smiled, and thought the better of Hurree
Babu, moved by like desire.

Rudyard Kipling, *Kim*

Sadler's Wells originated with the discovery in 1683 of a well in the garden of the Musick House built by businessman Richard Sadler. The area had been celebrated for its wells during the Middle Ages and the water was believed to have healing properties. Sadler, ever the entrepreneur, publicised his wells' amazing properties and by the end of the summer of 1685, hundreds of London's fashionable people were taking the waters. To entice and amuse his customers, Sadler added musicians, and, later, purpose-made buildings for the entertainment, and so its history began.

For many years the quality of the entertainment was mostly very poor; at its worst, the programme included a singing duck, a rope dancer and a man eating a live cockerel. It didn't help that the waters were used to brew beer to sell at the theatre, which was enjoyed more than the entertainment. Dickens, writing in 1851, found the theatre to be full of ruffians, who drank to excess and picked fights throughout the performance.

However, after decades of neglect, the theatre was finally saved by Lilian Baylis, director of the Old Vic, who set up a charitable foundation to buy Sadler's Wells for the nation. The new theatre duly opened on 6 January 1931 with a production of *Twelfth Night* and a cast headed by John Gielgud as Malvolio. Sir John was not impressed: 'How we all detested Sadler's Wells when it was opened first. The auditorium looked like a denuded wedding cake and the acoustics were dreadful.' Nevertheless, in the decades that followed, Sadler's Wells played host to some of the world's most outstanding performers of theatre, music and dance. On 30 June 1996, the last performance was given at the old theatre before it was demolished and rebuilt for the sixth time, in a gleaming reincarnation that is light years away from its dubious origins.

SPORTING LONDON

In 2002, the existing world record for the fastest female marathon runner was broken at the London Marathon by the UK's Paula Radcliffe, who ran the course in two hours, 15 minutes and 25 seconds. The world record had been broken in London twice before: in 1983, Greta Waitz of Norway clocked up two hours, 25 minutes and 29 seconds, and in 1985 Ingrid Christensen-Kristiansen of Norway completed the gruelling run in two hours, 21 minutes and six seconds. The world record for the fastest male marathon runner was also broken during the London Marathon, by Khalid Khannouchi of the USA, who in 2002 finished in two hours, five minutes and 38 seconds, beating his own record set in 1999 by four seconds.

CAPITAL CONUNDRUMS

Which five thoroughfares meet at Piccadilly Circus?
Answer on page 153.

LONDON SONGS

'London Calling' – *The Clash*
'London Nights' – *London Boys*
'London Kid' – *Jean Michel Jarre featuring Hank Marvin*
'A Nightingale Sang in Berkeley Square' – *Maschwitz and Sherwin*
'The Lambeth Walk' – *Rose, Furber and Gay*
'London Bridge is Falling Down' – *traditional nursery rhyme*
'Maybe It's Because I'm a Londoner' – *Hubert Gregg*
'Streets of London' – *Ralph McTell*
'London Town' – *Buck's Fizz*
'Waterloo Sunset' – *the Kinks*
'London's Burning' – *traditional nursery rhyme*
'Foggy Day in London Town' – *Ira and George Gershwin*
'Waterloo' – *Abba*

YOU CAN TAKE A HORSE TO WATER

Until 1859 it was very difficult for Londoners to find a drink of water without paying for it; and even more difficult for cart drivers and cabbies to find a watering-place for their horses. The only option was to use the troughs of water put out by publicans, but you had to pay a penny – or buy a beer. At this time, there were around 50,000 horses in constant use in the capital, which made a nice living for the pub-owners.

To solve the problem, Samuel Gurney, a member of parliament and well-known Quaker, set up the Metropolitan Free Drinking Fountain Association, opening the capital's first drinking fountain on 21 April 1859. This fountain can still be seen in the wall of St Sepulchre's Church in Newgate Street, EC1. More fountains were installed at a rate of about one a week for about two years, many of which incorporated small drinking-bowls for dogs.

Then in 1867 the Association expanded its activities to include horses and cattle, and changed its name to the Metropolitan Drinking Fountain and Cattle Trough Association. They installed large metal water troughs all over London, which were later replaced by granite, many of which survive today, as does the Association. It is now based in Kent, and installs drinking fountains in schools and playing fields, and works in other countries such as Africa to improve their access to water.

The number of offences punishable by death in London in 1722, which rose to 359 in the same year

I love London society! I think it has immensely improved. It is entirely composed now of beautiful idiots and brilliant lunatics. Just what Society should be.

Oscar Wilde, *An Ideal Husband, Act I*

SUGGESTIONS FOR A NEW USE
FOR THE MILLENNIUM DOME

Real suggestions made by potential purchasers plus a few ideas from members of the public...

Hi-tech business park
20,000-seat sports and entertainment venue
National football and athletics stadium to replace Wembley
Biotechnology centre
Sports academy or sports centre for public use
Ice rink
Nightclub (the Ministry of Sound held a New Year
party there at the end of 2000)
New housing development
Hospital
Add ears and a trunk and turn it into a white elephant

RIOTING IN THE STREETS

In June 1450, Jack Cade led tens of thousands of rebellious peasants to London to protest at the incompetence of King Henry VI and his government, unfair taxes, corruption and the recent loss of France. Alarmed, Henry fled to Warwickshire, leaving the city to its fate. The rebels took possession of Southwark, executed the Lord Treasurer and others, and, against Jack Cade's instructions, looted, robbed and raped at will. Captain Matthew Gough led a group of men to defeat the rioters, and a fierce battle was fought back and forth across London Bridge. Gough was killed, and the Lord Treasurer, Archbishop John Kemp, called for a truce; the rebels chose to leave with their plunder and a pardon, but Cade was soon hunted down and taken prisoner. He died on the way back to London, after which dozens more rebels were rounded up and executed.

LUVVERLY GRAPEFRUIT

Market trader Jack Smith was the first man to introduce the grapefruit to London when he sold it on his fruit stall in Berwick Street Market in 1890.

Subterranean relics of London's history

Relic	Underneath where?
Norman crypt	Church of St Bartholomew the Great, Smithfield
Norman crypt	Church of St Mary-le-Bow
Remains of Giltspur Street Compter (debtor's prison)	Viaduct Tavern, EC4
Medieval cellars	The Olde Cheshire Cheese, Fleet Street
Thirteenth century crypt	Sequestered St Etheldreda, Ely Place EC1
Thirteenth century crypt	Guildhall, EC2
Eighteenth century Roman style plunge bath	Strand Lane
Artesian well	Harrods
Underground tunnels and cellars plus a cell for shoplifters	Harrods
Remains of the Clerkenwell House of Detention	Clerkenwell
190 miles of shelving holding 12 million books	British Library, Euston Road
Carlo Gatti's ice wells, c.1860	King's Cross (London Canal Museum)
Room from a prior's house, c.1420	Whitefriars Street, Britton's Court
Twelfth century crypt	All Hallows Staining
Full-sized steam train	Wembley Stadium (it was part of an abandoned building scheme)
Boadicea's grave	A platform at King's Cross (according to one of many legends about where she is buried)
A never-completed Tube station	1 Hampstead Way

IS THAT YOUR BAG?

In 1998, Anthony Noel Kelly was convicted of stealing body parts from the Royal College of Surgeons, which he used to make moulds for sculptures at his Shepherd's Bush studio. The story would have been disturbing enough without the added detail that Neil Lindsay, the embalmer who helped Kelly to procure the body parts, transported the human remains to Shepherd's Bush by tube and taxi, wrapped in black dustbin bags. The crime might have been overlooked had Kelly not divulged his methods to an arts journalist in 1996, shortly after which he was arrested.

Trundling underneath London, Tube passengers occasionally find themselves passing through abandoned stations, with dusty, unused platforms and dimly flickering lights. And it might be one of these...

Aldgate East: Opened October 1884, on the north side of Whitechapel High Street. When the line was electrified, the platforms were too short for the new, longer cars, which caused delays as passengers had to walk through to the next carriage. A new Aldgate East was built, and the old one closed in 1938.

Aldwych: located on the Strand near Surrey Street, it used to run special trains every night to take theatregoers home. Reroutings meant that the line became little used, and when the lifts needed replacing in September 1994 at a cost of £3 million, it was closed.

British Museum: Situated on the north side of High Holborn, this should have interchanged with the line at Holborn, but a proposed subway connection was never built and passengers had to connect at street level. The new central line at Holborn in 1933 rendered the station redundant and it was closed in 1933.

Brompton Road: Rather too close to South Kensington and Knightsbridge, the station was unpopular, and eventually drivers were ordered to drive through it out of rush hour, which gave rise to the cry 'Passing Brompton Road', also the name of a 1928 play. Closed in July 1934.

City Road: At the junction of City Road and Moreland Street, between Old Street and Angel stations, this closed in 1922 while improvements were made, but never reopened. Converted to an air raid shelter in 1941, but abandoned after the war.

Down Street: Opened 1903 between Green Park and Hyde Park Corner, this was too close to both, and tucked away off the main street in an area where residents had little use for the Tube. Closed in 1932.

King William Street: On the corner of King William Street and Arthur Street East, its opening was attended by the Prince of Wales (later Edward VII), who luckily was not on board when the train broke down on its return journey. The station was badly designed and after many alterations it was closed in 1900.

South Kentish Town: Between Camden Town and Kentish Town on the Northern Line, this was closed during a power cut and never reopened. A passenger once managed to alight at the closed station, and had to wait for another train to stop and pick him up. The incident inspired John Betjeman to write a short story, *South Kentish Town*, which he broadcast on the BBC.

SPORTING LONDON

The original pitch for the Oval cricket ground in Kennington consisted of 10,000 squares of turf cut from Tooting Common.

WHO NAMED THE THAMES?

No name is recorded for London's main river before Julius Caesar referred to it as Tamesis. After 'Kent', this is the oldest place name in England.

THE PRESIDENTIAL BUNKER

In *Subterranean City*, Antony Clayton explains how, during World War Two, General Eisenhower was made to feel at home with his very own underground shelter. A number of deep-level shelters were built during the war to offer protection from air-raids, and part of the bunker at Goodge Street station was offered to the General in 1942 for his exclusive use. Eisenhower installed a direct phone line to the Cabinet War Rooms (also underground) and used the Goodge Street shelter as his signal centre during the Normandy landings. However, he actually slept at the Dorchester, which had a gas-proof reinforced concrete basement. After Eisenhower had vacated the shelter, it was used to house British troops on their way to various overseas territories such as Cyprus and Singapore. A fire in 1956 meant that it was abandoned for a while, but in the 1980s it was leased to a security company as a storage facility. By 1992, it held tapes of the entire output of Channel 4. The glass mercury arc rectifier that helped to provide emergency lighting was once used to represent an alien brain in an episode of 'Dr Who'.

LONDON WORDS

On the subject of Sir Thomas More
After he was beheaded, his trunke was interred in Chelsey church, neer the middle of the South wall, where was some slight Monument erected. His head was upon London bridge. There goes this story in the family, viz. that one day as one of his daughters was passing under the Bridge, looking on her father's head, sayd she, That head haz layn many a time in my Lapp, would to God it would fall into my Lap as I passe under. She had her wish, and it did fall into her Lappe, and is now preserved in a vault in the Cathedral Church at Canterbury.
John Aubrey, Brief Lives

It is the gondola of London.
Benjamin Disraeli, on the London hansom cab

LET ME TAKE YOU UNDER
THE STREETS OF LONDON

In December 1980, journalist Duncan Campbell took an unusual walk from East London to Westminster – underground. In a report for the *New Statesman*, he climbed (illegally) down an access shaft in Bethnal Green Road 100 feet below the surface to a well-lit tunnel and set off to Westminster by bicycle. What he found was an extraordinary and extensive network of well-maintained tunnels below the city centre. His route at first converged with the Central line tube tunnel, the Mail Rail tunnel (exclusively used by the Post Office) and another tunnel that led to an underground telephone exchange near St Paul's. Campbell didn't need a map, as there were frequent signposts to places of interest such as Whitehall, The Mall and Lord's Cricket Ground.

The tunnels led, among other places, to Holborn, Covent Garden, Fleet Street, Leicester Square, the Post Office Tower, Waterloo and, of course, to Whitehall. Campbell found another telephone exchange just south of Nelson's Column, from where he could have reached (by lift) the Ministry of Defence, the Treasury, the Admiralty and Downing Street. He finally emerged back in the Holborn Telephone Exchange, near to the *New Statesman's* offices. It is also rumoured (not surprisingly) that there are tunnels from Buckingham Palace to Parliament and Wellington Barracks, whose presence is hinted at by a mysterious extractor fan placed outside the ICA on the Mall, as well as a set of steps that can be seen by peering through a louvred window in the ICA gents' toilets.

SIGNIFICANT STATUES

Eleanor's crosses
When Eleanor of Castile, the queen of Edward I, died suddenly in 1290, she was commemorated by her grieving spouse by a series of 12 gothic stone spires. One spire was placed at each spot where her funeral cortege rested on its journey from Nottinghamshire, where she died, to Westminster Abbey, where she was buried. Only two of the original crosses survive, in Hertfordshire and Northampton. The last of Eleanor's crosses was erected at Charing Cross, but the spire that is there now is a nineteenth-century replacement.

I LEFT IT ON THE BUS

A few things left behind on London Transport in the last year

24,084 cases and bags
20,846 books
10,614 mobile phones
7,505 sets of keys
7,026 umbrellas
6,118 pairs of spectacles
2,671 pairs of gloves
474 single gloves
a 14-foot boat
a wedding dress
an urn filled with ashes
several lawyers' robes
a briefcase containing £10,000
false teeth, limbs and eyes
2.5 hundredweight of
dried fruit
a lawnmower

a Chinese typewriter
breast implants
a theatrical coffin
a stuffed eagle
a divan bed
an outboard motor
a park bench
a grandfather clock
a bishop's crook
a garden slide
a jar of bull's sperm
three dead bats in a container
a stuffed puffa fish
a vasectomy kit
a harpoon gun
two human skulls in a bag
a kitchen sink

Over 133,000 items are found every year, between 500 and 600 every day. If an item is not picked up by its owner within three months (money is kept for 12 months), it is sold and the proceeds go towards the running costs of the Lost Property Office.

NICE WORK IF YOU CAN GET IT

A popular way to earn money in late eighteenth-century London was to dig up dead bodies. A freshly retrieved body could fetch up to £4, or less for a 'short' (a child), the corpses of which were priced by the foot. The gravediggers were known as 'resurrection men' and while their victims were unresisting, the body burglars did run the risk of being caught by spring guns, primitive landmines and other booby traps set up by the grieving relatives. The favoured method for a 'resurrection' was to dig a small hole down to the coffin, break the coffin lid and drag the body up through the narrow opening, rather than dig up the entire grave, which took time and attracted more attention. Inevitably, some resurrection men resorted to murder to speed up the process, such as James May and John Bishop. The two bodysnatchers were arrested in 1831 after arguing over the price of a body supplied to King's College Hospital, which turned out to be that of a street urchin they had murdered. They were hanged, and their bodies dissected by surgeons.

LONDON FOOTBALL CLUBS

Name	Date founded	Highest position reached
Arsenal	1886	Champions in Division One and Premier League
Brentford	1889	5th in Division One
Charlton	1905	2nd in Division One
Chelsea	1905	Champions in Division One
Crystal Palace	1905	3rd in Division One
Fulham	1879	Champions in Division One
Leyton Orient	1881	22nd in Division One
Millwall	1885	3rd in Division One
Queen's Park Rangers	1885	2nd in Division One
Spurs	1882	Champions in Division One
West Ham	1900	3rd in Division One
Wimbledon	1889	6th in Division One and Premier League

QUOTE UNQUOTE

London, that great cesspool into which all the loungers and idlers of the Empire are irresistibly drained.
Sir Arthur Conan Doyle, writer

LONDON WORDS

On Monday the first of May, 1826, the first anniversary dinner of the United Society of Master Chimney Sweepers' took place at the Eyre Tavern, St John's Wood, Marylebone.

About eleven o'clock, two hundred of their apprentices proceeded in great regularity through the principal streets and squares at the west end of the town, accompanied by an excellent band of music. The clean and wholesome appearance of the lads, certainly, reflected much credit on their masters...the boys were regaled with a substantial repast of roast beef and plum pudding; after which the masters themselves sat down to a very excellent dinner provided for the occasion...

Mr Bennett, of Welbeck Street, addressed the company on the subject of cleansing chimneys with the machine, the introduction of which he was confident would never answer the intended purposes. He urged the absolute necessity of climbing boys in their trade; and instanced several cases in which the machines were rendered perfectly useless: most of the chimneys in the great houses at the west end of the town were constructed in such a manner that it was utterly impossible to clear them of soot, unless a human being was sent up for that purpose.

William Hone's *Table Book*, 1826

*When Lucy asked Charles to take her to the Ritz tea dance,
he had no idea what he was letting himself in for*

SALE OF THE CENTURY

One of the most talked-about auctions in the history of Sotheby's in
London was the Goldschmidt sale of 1958. The Goldschmidt collection contained seven of the most exquisite Impressionist and Modern
paintings ever to come to auction. The auction house decided to
revive an eighteenth century tradition and hold an evening auction, at
which the attendants were required to wear evening dress. Fourteen
hundred people attended, including W Somerset Maugham, Anthony
Quinn, Kirk Douglas and Lady Churchill, as well as art dealers from
all over the world. All seven pictures were sold in just 21 minutes and
fetched £781,000, the highest total ever achieved at the time for a fine
art sale. The highest price was paid for Cézanne's *Garçon au Gilet
Rouge*, which was sold for £220,000, more than five times the price
ever paid for a painting sold at auction. The Goldschmidt sale was
one of the social highlights of the year.

CAPITAL CONUNDRUMS

Who is Great Tom, and what does he have to do with Big Ben?
Answer on page 153.

IMPRESSIONS OF LONDON

Famous paintings of the capital

Lucian Freud ....*Factory in North London* 1972
Joseph Mallord William Turner ....*London,* 1809
James McNeill Whistler ....*London Bridge,* 1885
James McNeill Whistler ....*Nocturne in Blue and Gold:*
Old Battersea Bridge, 1872-1875
Hans Holbein the Younger...........................*Georg Gisze, a German,*
merchant in London, 1532
Camille Pissarro ....*Hyde Park, London,* 1890
Camille Pissarro ....*Charing Cross Bridge, London,* 1890
James Tissot ....*London Visitors,* c.1874

PUB QUIZ

Notorious London pubs

The Magdala, Hampstead
Ruth Ellis shot her lover, David Blakely, outside this pub in 1955
and, when convicted, became the last woman to be hanged
in England.

The Goat, Kensington
Murderer John George Haigh met his first victim, William
McSwann, here before luring him off, killing him and dissolving his
body in a bath of acid.

The Bow Tavern
This now demolished pub on St Giles High Street was where
condemned prisoners stopped for their last pint of ale on their way
from Newgate Prison to Tyburn Gallows (now Marble Arch). If the
executioner rode on the same cart, he was not allowed a drink –
hence the phrase 'on the wagon'.

Blind Beggar, Whitechapel Road
Where Ronnie Kray's murdered one of his many enemies, George
Cornell, by shooting him through the eye. By strange coincidence,
given the pub's name, this was also where Bulldog Wallis, a
pickpocket and ruffian, killed a man by pushing an umbrella tip
through his eye.

On 30 April 1980, six Iranian dissidents seized the Iranian Embassy in Prince's Gate, SW1, overpowering the unfortunate constable who stood guard at the door. The six armed men claimed to be from the Democratic Revolutionary Front for Arabistan, and seized the embassy to protest against the oppression of Iran by Ayatollah Khomeini, and to secure the release of 91 imprisoned comrades. Twenty-six people were held hostage for six days, consisting mostly of embassy staff, but including two BBC journalists who had stopped by to pick up visas and got the scoop of a lifetime, though were powerless to do much at the time. Initially the siege was peaceful; some hostages were released, including a pregnant woman and BBC journalist Chris Cramer, who, with the agreement of his fellow hostages, exaggerated a stomach complaint in order to be released. Once out, he provided the SAS with crucial information about the hostage-takers and the layout of the building. The siege dragged on for five long days, but when an Iranian hostage was shot and his body pushed outside, the SAS went in. The storming of the embassy has earned its place in history largely because it took place on Bank Holiday Monday, and was watched live on television by an enthralled public. It was all over in 15 minutes; five of the gunmen and another hostage was killed. PC Trevor Lock, who had been on guard outside and was one of the hostages – was awarded the George Cross for tackling one of the gunmen. The Iranian Embassy remained closed for years while the Iranian and British governments wrangled over who would pay for the damage to the building. It finally reopened in 1993. The five gunmen were buried in Woodgrange Park, Manor Park, in an unmarked grave.

WE'RE JUST MOVING HOUSE

In 1947, a new Ministry of Defence building was scheduled for construction just off Whitehall. The only snag was that underneath the site was a wine cellar once owned by Cardinal Wolsey, measuring 32 feet in width, and 20 feet in height. The building could not continue while it remained, so rather than destroy it, the entire cellar was temporarily moved out of the way, lock, stock and (appropriately) barrel. The 1000-tonne structure was placed on a concrete platform, which in turn rested on 200 steel rollers. The whole was then gently shifted 43 feet and six inches to the west. The site was excavated by a further 20 feet, and the cellar was rolled back into place, and came to rest in its original location, 20 feet lower down. The whole process took around two and a half years.

Snow falls in the buffet of Aldersgate station,
Soot hangs in the tunnel in clouds of steam.
City of London! before the next desecration
Let your steepled forest of churches be my theme.

Sunday Silence! with every street a dead street,
Alley and courtyard empty and cobbled mews,
Till 'tingle tang' the bell of St Mildred's Bread Street
Summoned the sermon taster to high box pews,

And neighbouring towers and spirelets joined the ringing
With answering echoes from heavy commercial walls
Till all were drowned as the sailing clouds went singing
On the roaring flood of a twelve-voiced peal from Paul's.

Then would the years fall off and Thames run slowly,
Out into marshy meadow-land flowed the Fleet,
And the walled-in City of London, smelly and holy,
Had a tinkling mass house in every cavernous street.

The bells rang down and St Michael Paternoster
Would take me into its darkness from College Hill,
Or Christ Church Newgate Street (with St Leonard Foster)
Would be late for Mattins and ringing insistent still.

Last of the east wall sculpture, a cherub gazes
On broken arches, rosebay, bracken and dock,
Where once I heard the roll of the Prayer Book phrases
And the sumptuous tick of the old west gallery clock.

Snow falls in the buffet of Aldersgate station,
Toiling and doomed from Moorgate Street puffs the train
For us of the steam and the gas-light, the lost generation,
The new white cliffs of the City are built in vain.

Sir John Betjeman, Poet Laureate
Monody on the Death of Aldersgate Street Station

QUOTE UNQUOTE

*Far too neat. These people seem to have died with
white gloves on.*
Gustave Flaubert, novelist, commenting on the graves
in Highgate Cemetery

IRA BOMBS IN LONDON

8 March 1973	Old Bailey and Scotland Yard, 1 killed, 174 hurt
10 September 1973	King's Cross, five hurt
10 September 1973	Euston Station, eight hurt
22 October 1974	Brooks Club, three hurt
17 June 1974	Houses of Parliament, 11 hurt
17 July 1974	Tower of London, one killed, 41 injured
5 September 1975	London Hilton, two killed, 63 injured
9 October 1975	Green Park tube station, one killed, 20 injured
12 November 1975	Scott's Restaurant, one killed
18 November 1975	Walton's Restaurant, two killed, 23 injured
29 January 1976	12 bombs planted, including Selfridges, one hurt
30 March 1979	Airey Neave MP killed by car bomb in House of Commons car park
20 July 1982	Hyde Park and Regents Park: 11 killed, 50 injured, seven horses killed
17 December 1983	Harrods, six killed, 75 injured
20 July 1990	Stock Exchange, none hurt
10 April 1992	Baltic Exchange, three killed
24 April 1993	Bishopsgate, one killed, 44 injured
9 February 1996	Canary Wharf, two killed, 39 injured
3 March 2001	BBC news centre, one injured
6 May 2001	Hendon Post Office, one injured
3 August 2001	Ealing Broadway, seven injured

MIXED SIGNALS

Until 1750 there were only two ways to cross the Thames, over London Bridge or on the horse-ferry between Lambeth and Millbank. However there were plenty of enterprising boatmen willing to row you across for a small fee. They would row up and down the Thames, calling out 'Oars! Oars!' to passers-by, which worked perfectly well with London residents. However, visitors from more rural areas were inclined to mistake this offer for something less savoury, as they assumed that the boatmen were dropping their aitches.

QUOTE UNQUOTE

All that changing of plates and flapping of napkins while you wait 40 minutes for your food.
Sir Hugh Casson, architect, on London restaurants

LENIN WAS HERE

Russian revolutionary Lenin took refuge in London in the early 1900s, finding safety at the following addresses:

22 Ampton Street: where the 2nd Congress of the Russian Social-Democratic Labour Party was held

British Library Reading Room: where he signed in as Jacob Richter and worked at seat L13

14 Frederick Street: his London mailing address

26 Granville Square: where the editorial board of the revolutionary newspaper *Iskra* met

30 Holford Square: his first London address, where he and his wife posed as the Jacob Richters

16 Percy Circus: his home on his second visit to London in 1905, to attend the 3rd Congress of the Russian Social-Democratic Labour Party

20 Regent Square: used by *Iskra* as a mailing address

36 Tavistock Place: lived here in 1908 to carry out research at the British Library

37A Clerkenwell Place: Lenin worked on *Iskra* at the Twentieth Century Press at this address until April 1903. The press was set up by William Morris.

PAY UP ALL YE WHO PASS

This list of charges for the tollgate at Alleyn's College of God's Gift in Dulwich remains on display, although the toll is no longer charged:

For every motor car, motorcycle or motorcycle combination	6d
For every van, lorry or other commercial vehicle under one tonne laden weight	6d
For every van, lorry or other commercial vehicle from one to five tonnes laden weight	2/6
For every horse, mule or donkey not drawing	3d
For every horse, mule or donkey drawing any vehicle	6d
For beasts per score and so on in proportion for any less number	10d
For sheep, lambs or hogs per score in proportion (but not less than 1/2d) for any less number	21/2d

HELLO SAILOR

If you come across a sailor with a strange bulge in his pocket, fear not; a superstition that originated in the London docks in 1917 means that sailors used to carry a pincushion as a charm against drowning.

London's inventors and their most famous achievements

Edmund Halley was the first Astronomer Royal at Greenwich, and the first person to **calculate a comet's orbit**. He predicted that a comet seen in 1682 would reappear in 1758. Sadly he died before he saw it proved, but it did reappear on cue and was named after him.

In 1837, William Fothergill Cooke and Professor Charles Wheatstone patented a five-needle **telegraph**. On 25 July, Wheatstone's and Cooke's telegraph was demonstrated to the directors of the London and Birmingham Railway between Euston and Camden Town, a distance of just under a mile. In 1839 the world's first commercial telegraph line using the Cooke and Wheatstone system was built between Paddington and West Drayton, a distance of 13 miles. It was working to Hanwell by the 6 April and was completed to West Drayton on 9 April. The public could pay one shilling to view the telegraph and could send their own telegrams. In 1845 the first public telegraph line was opened and ran between London and Gosport. The first communication transmitted was Queen Victoria's speech at the opening of Parliament.

Michael Faraday discovered (among other things) **electromagnetic rotation**, and built the first electric motor, generator and transformer.

Hiram Maxim invented the **automatic machine gun** in his workshop in Hatton Garden. Patented in 1883, it could fire up to 600 rounds a minute. He also invented a locomotive headlight and a set of curling tongs, among 100 other ideas.

The first **British-built petrol-driven internal combustion engine car** was built by Frederick Bremer at his home in Walthamstow, and first took to the road in 1892. The car can be seen at the Vestry House Museum, E17.

On 27 July 1896, Guglielmo Marconi went up on to the roof of the GPO North building on King Edward Street to test his apparatus for transmitting electrical impulses through the air. It was the first demonstration of **radio waves**.

John Logie Baird first demonstrated the **television** on 26 January 1926 at 22 Frith Street W1, in a room above what is now Bar Italia.

Alexander Fleming discovered **penicillin** at St Mary's Hospital in Paddington on 3 September 1928. He discovered it by accident while looking for a chemical that could stop infection.

Charles Darwin (1809–82), formed his **evolutionary theory** and wrote *The Origin of Species* (1859) while living in London.

Bringing his own costume to set, Richard Gere clearly hadn't properly read the script of An Officer and a Gentleman.

LONDON LEGENDS

William Caxton

William Caxton (c.1422–c.1491) was the founder of British printing. Born in Kent, he was a textile merchant's apprentice in London, but upon the death of his master he moved to Bruges and opened his own textile business. He became the governor of the Merchant Adventurers, which meant that he travelled extensively and spoke Dutch and French and became an accomplished translator. Caxton went to Cologne to study the printing technique developed by Gutenberg, and when he returned to London in 1476, he opened a printing press in Westminster, London. It is thought that *Dictes or Sayengis of the Philosophres* was the first book that he printed on this press, which was published on 18 November 1477, the first book published in Britain. Caxton published about 100 works, including Geoffrey Chaucer's *Troilus and Criseyde* and *The Canterbury Tales*. One of these first editions of *The Canterbury Tales* was sold for £4.6 million in 1998. When Caxton died, his assistant, Wynandus van Woerden, better known as Wynkyn de Worde, continued the business, and eventually set up his own printing press in 1500 on Shoe Lane near Fleet Street, thus establishing a centuries-long tradition for that area as being the heart of the British newspaper industry.

The day of the Victory March, 1919

That night London went mad, but the most part of it was a decent joyous madness without vice in it. I was caught up in the surging crowds who linked arms and were cheering and singing. Outside Buckingham Palace they called for the King time and time again, and he had come out to his balcony, with the Queen and his family, smiling down on this vast multitude, raising his hand to them. At night I found myself in Pall Mall, with sore feet which had been trodden on many times. A soldier, just a little drunk, was on the pedestal of Florence Nightingale's statue, with his arm round the figure of that lady. He was making a speech to which no one listened except myself. Over and over again he assured the crowds that the bloody war wouldn't have been won without the help of women like good old Florence. 'It's the women of England who won the war', he shouted, 'and that's the bloody truth of it!' No one challenged this statement.

No one listened except me, curious to know what he was saying with such fervour and passion. I never pass the statue of Florence Nightingale now without thinking of that champion of womanhood who was a little drunk.

Philip Gibbs, *The Pageant of the Years*

CAPITAL CONUNDRUMS

Where is the Chicken Run?
Answer on page 153.

RIOTING IN THE STREETS

On 4 October 1936, Oswald Mosley set off to lead a crowd of anti-Jewish protesters from the Tower of London to the East End, to mark the fourth anniversary of the founding of the British Union of Fascists. Two thousand BUF supporters, known as Blackshirts, congregated around Cable Street, while 500 anti-fascists assembled at the end of Whitechapel High Street to block their way and shouted 'They shall not pass!' Both sides surged towards each other, carrying crude weapons made of bits of wood, and the anti-Fascists overturning vehicles to impede the blackshirts progress. By 3pm the clash had become a pitched battle, with some of the most vicious street fighting ever seen in London. Mosley joined the battle in his Bentley, surrounded by muscled bodyguards. The crowds were eventually dispersed, though not before Mosley made a speech, accusing the government of surrendering to Jewish corruption. The government banned the BUF in 1940 and Mosley was interned for most of the rest of the war. He never successfully returned to politics and eventually moved to France.

TUNNEL VISION

In October 1940 the government agreed to build eight deep-level shelters, which was eventually increased to 10, at Clapham South, Clapham Common, Clapham North, Stockwell, Oval, St Paul's, Chancery Lane, Goodge Street, Camden Town and Belsize Park. They would be built 85-105 feet deep, and access would be by a shaft sunk at either end of the tunnel, with staircases separate to the existing ones, emerging in above-level block houses made from reinforced concrete.

Not all of the proposed stations were built – Oval and St Paul's were abandoned – but the block-houses for the remaining shelters can still be seen. After the war it was suggested that the deep tunnels be used to create an express Northern line service, running non-stop into the West End. Sadly, as Northern Line regulars can attest, this idea was never developed.

SIGNIFICANT STATUES

Albert Memorial

The Albert Memorial is the Taj Mahal of London – a gesture of undying love from a bereft spouse. When Queen Victoria's beloved husband Prince Albert died of typhoid aged just 41, the queen was so devastated that she went into mourning for many years. She commissioned Sir George Gilbert Scott to design a fabulous memorial so that Albert would never be forgotten, and Scott came up with a 175 foot overwrought, gothic edifice, with a black and gilded spire, marble canopy, mosaics, enamels, wrought iron and hundreds of sculpted figures. The steps that lead up to the prince are guarded by figures that represent Europe, Africa, America and Asia – thus the grieving widow had placed the world at her beloved's feet.

PROBLEM PENSIONERS

In *Brewer's Rogues, Villains and Eccentrics*, William Donaldson relates the sorry tale of pensioner Sid Chaney who in 1994 opened an account at Barclays Bank in Camden Town in the name of his ferret, improbably called Sir Andrew Large. Chaney then opened another account at the City branch of the NatWest Bank in N1 in the name of Mr Sniffles, his cat, and another in the name of his budgerigar, Captain Mainwaring. Easily escaping the attentions of the banks' security procedures, in no time at all he and his pets ran up a debt of £117,000. On the one occasion when a vetting procedure would have been appropriate, it was conspicuous by its absence. Mr Chaney escaped prosecution except by American Express, whose debt of £11,500 he is paying off at £1 a week, which should take him 230 years.

OLD PICTURE, NEW CAPTION

When the 8.32 to Clapham Junction became unreasonably overcrowded, Jeremy took matters into his own hands.

LONDON WORDS

Algernon Stitch went to his office in a sombre and rather antiquated Daimler; Julia always drove herself, in the latest model of mass-produced baby car; brand-new twice a year, painted an invariable brilliant black, tiny and glossy as a midget's funeral hearse. She mounted the kerb and bowled rapidly along the pavement to the corner of St James's, where a policeman took her number and ordered her into the road.

'Third time this week,' said Mrs Stitch. 'I wish they wouldn't. It's such a nuisance for Algy.'

Once embedded in the traffic block, she stopped the engine and turned her attention to the crossword.

'It's "detonated",' she said, filling it in.

...Eight minutes close application was enough to finish the puzzle. Mrs Stitch folded the paper and tossed it over her shoulder into the back seat; looked about her resentfully at the stationary traffic.

'This is too much,' she said; started the engine, turned sharp again on to the kerb and proceeded to Piccadilly, driving before her at a brisk pace, until he took refuge on the step of Brooks's, a portly, bald young man; when he reached safety, he turned to remonstrate, recognized Mrs Stitch, and bowed profoundly to the tiny, black back as it shot the corner of Arlington Street. 'One of the things I like about these absurd cars,' she said, 'is that you can do things with them that you couldn't do in a real one.'

Evelyn Waugh, *Scoop*

SIGNIFICANT STATUES

Monument is the tallest freestanding stone column in the world, measuring 202 feet high, and stands 202 feet from the site of the baker's house in Pudding Lane where the Great Fire of London began in 1666. The column was designed as a commemoration of the Great Fire by Robert Hooke and Christopher Wren, the two men responsible for rebuilding much of London after the devastating conflagration. Made of Portland stone, it took six years to build and was completed in 1677. The ornament for the top is a simple copper urn with gilt flames, which was chosen in preference to Wren's earlier suggestions of a phoenix and a statue of Charles II (the King himself preferred the urn). Inside is a cantilevered stone staircase around a central well with 311 steps leading to a viewing platform 160 feet (50 metres) above ground level. The platform became a popular spot for a number of suicides, and was finally enclosed in 1842. The steps continue inside the pillar above the platform, and there is a vertical ladder through the urn to a trapdoor at the very top of the Monument.

What most people don't know is that the Monument was also designed as the setting for a series of experiments that required a structure of some height, and Hooke and Wren included a cellar laboratory below the ground floor. Hooke wanted to use the tower to experiment with a zenith telescope, which would make exact measurements of a selected fixed star. The hollow shaft could be opened to the night sky by a hinged trapdoor in the urn at the top, while the experimenter took up his position in the cellar laboratory.

In addition, the steps were built so that each stair-riser was exactly six inches high, which meant the tower could be used for experiments on pressure, while the vertical shaft could be used for experiments with pendulums. Hooke duly recorded a number of experiments carried out at the 'Fish Street pillar'. Twenty-first century visitors can still climb to the viewing platform, though the laboratory and the steps up through the urn are out of bounds.

QUOTE UNQUOTE

The Englishman's telephone box is his castle. Like the London taxi, it can be entered by a gentleman in a top hat. It protects the user's privacy, keeps him warm and is large enough for a small cocktail party.
Mary Blume, protesting at the replacement of Britain's bright-red phone boxes in the *International Herald Tribune*, 1985

The granting of the Freedom of the City is one of London's oldest surviving traditions, dating back to the early thirteenth century. A freeman was someone who was not the property of a feudal lord and enjoyed certain privileges such as the right to earn money and own land, essential for anyone who wanted to practise a trade. Freemen enjoyed a number of other privileges, although many were assumed rather than enshrined in law. These included the right:

- to herd sheep over London bridge
- to carry a drawn sword in the City
- to avoid being press-ganged
- to be married in St Paul's Cathedral
- to be buried in the City
- to be drunk and disorderly without fear of arrest
- if convicted of a suitable offence, to be hanged with a silken rope
- if their children were orphaned, to have them educated free of charge at the Freeman's School in Kent
- if they became destitute in old age, to be housed in an almshouse

The freedom of the city is still granted to around 1,800 people a year who meet the criteria, which include being the child or the apprentice of a freeman, or being nominated, usually by the Livery company to which the candidate belongs. In addition, the Corporation of London can invite certain people to be an Honorary Freeman, an honour most recently bestowed upon Winston Churchill, General Eisenhower, Nelson Mandela, cricketer Darren Gough and the late Princess of Wales (female freemen are referred to as 'free sisters').

Although only the last two of the special privileges listed above still apply, the others can be invoked from time to time for a good cause. On 12 December 1983, newly elected Freeman Michael Bradshaw exercised his ancient right to drive a flock of sheep over London Bridge. Despite his flat cap, Mr Bradshaw was in fact the director of an advertising company, and the stunt was in aid of the National Advertising Benevolent Society.

TAKE TEN PACES...

St James's Street, London SW1, opens out through onto the historic Pickering Place – not only the smallest public square in Great Britain with original gas lighting, but also the square in which the last duel in Great Britain was fought. A plaque on the wall erected by the Anglo-Texan Society indicates that from 1842–45 a building here was occupied by the Legation from Republic of Texas to the Court of St James's.

LONDON ON LOCATION

Films shot in Trafalgar Square

- *101 Dalmatians* (1996): Joely Richardson cycles through the square with her dog
- *Arabesque* (1966): director Stanley Donen used a camera mounted on Nelson's Column
- *Honest* (2000): the All Saints turn to crime
- *The Day the Earth Caught Fire* (1961): a CND rally takes place in Trafalgar Square
- *It Happened Here* (1964): a Nazi rally is held in the Square
- *The Avengers* (1998): Fiona Shaw and Uma Thurman crash their getaway balloon into a road sign as they fly over a snowy Trafalgar Square
- *28 Days Later* (2002): apocalyptic thriller features an eerily deserted Square

LONDON PHRASES

London paste – a paste made of caustic soda and unslacked lime; used as to destroy tumours.

London pride – a garden name for *Saxifraga umbrosa*, a hardy perennial herbaceous plant, a native of high lands in Great Britain. (b) A name anciently given to the Sweet William. Also known as none-so-pretty and St Patrick's Cabbage.

London rocket – a cruciferous plant (*Sisymbrium irio*) which sprung up all over London out of the ruins of the Great Fire.

London clay – a geological formation in the lower division of the Eocene in SE England.

London plane – a hybrid plane tree, resistant to smoke and therefore often planted in streets.

London broil – in the US this is a mixed grill; in the UK it was a boneless cut of beef (as from the shoulder or flank) usually served sliced diagonally across the grain.

London Rules – boxing rules introduced in 1838 to prevent unfair play such as gouging and headbutting during bare-knuckle fighting; however, they were largely ignored, and London rules is usually meant as a euphemism for 'no rules'.

London forces – a synonym for van der Waals' forces, first postulated by van der Waals in 1873 to explain deviations from ideal gas behaviour seen in real gases.

London dispersion forces – the forces that exist in nonpolar molecules that involve an accidental dipole that induces a momentary dipole in a neighbour.

London Particular – thick blankets of fog that choked London's air until the Clean Air act was introduced; also the name of a recipe for thick pea and ham soup; and the subtitle of a small London fanzine, *Smoke: A London Particular.*

QUOTE UNQUOTE

*London...remains a man's city where New York is chiefly a
woman's. London has whole streets that cater to men's wants. It has
its great solid phalanx of fortress clubs.*
Louis Kronenberger, US critic and editor

GOING UNDERGROUND

The map of the London Underground, one of London's most recognisable icons, was created by a 28-year-old draughtsman called Henry Beck, who in 1931 was laid off from his job. Short of things to do, he fell to thinking about the Tube map and how it might be improved; at the time it was based on a street map, and was geographically more accurate than the current version. Beck redrew it with three principles in mind: that it should be a diagram rather than a map; that the centre should be enlarged in proportion to the outskirts for greater clarity; and that every line should be either vertical, horizontal or a 45-degree diagonal. The resulting map was clear, simple to understand and a work of graphic genius. Needless to say, his superiors disagreed at first, but fortunately he persuaded them to print 500 copies as a trial. It was an instant success, and by 1933 had completely replaced its predecessor. Beck continued to refine his map, although it took him 16 years to hit on the idea of using a white circle and connecting line to show where stations interchanged. Beck's final edition was printed in 1959, after which his name was removed and the map is now copyrighted to London Regional Transport. But his work will never be forgotten.

HIPPOS IN THE THAMES

Eighteen thousand years ago, during the last glacial episode of the Ice Age, most of Britain was covered by ice, during which time woolly mammoths roamed the Thames Valley. At the peak of the Ice Age, the sea-level was 120 metres lower than it is now, and the English Channel and most of the North Sea were land. The Ice Age consisted of glacial and interglacial cycles, and during the interglacials, it was warm enough for hippopotamus, hyena and lions to live in the area that is now London. Hippopotamus bones were discovered during the building of the National Gallery.

CAPITAL CONUNDRUMS

Why is the spire of St Bride's eight feet shorter than it should be?
Answer on page 153.

ORIGINAL NAMES OF TUBE STATIONS

Underground stations have often lost their original names; here are a few of the more familiar ones

Original name	Details	Current name
Aldersgate Street	Renamed Aldersgate & Barbican in 1923, then Barbican in 1968	Barbican
Bishopsgate	Renamed in 1909	Liverpool Street
Brentford Road	Renamed in 1906	Gunnersbury
Brompton (Gloucester Road)	Renamed in 1907	Gloucester Road
Clapham Road	Renamed in 1926	Clapham North
Dover Street	Renamed in 1933	Green Park
Eastcheap	Renamed in 1884	Monument
Euston Road	Renamed 1908	Warren Street
Farringdon Street	Renamed Farringdon & High Holborn in 1922, then became Farringdon in 1936	Farringdon
Gillespie Road	Renamed in 1932	Arsenal
Gower Street	Renamed in 1909	Euston Square
Great Central	Renamed in 1917	Marylebone
Highgate	Renamed Archway (Highgate) in 1939, Highgate (Archway) in 1941 and finally Archway in 1947	Archway
Kennington Road	Renamed Westminster Bridge Road in 1906, then Lambeth North in 1917	Lambeth North
Mark Lane	Renamed 1946	Tower Hill
Mill Hill Park	Renamed in 1910	Acton Town
North End (Fulham)	Renamed 1877	West Kensington
Notting Hill & Ladbroke Grove	Renamed Ladbroke Grove (North Kensington) in 1919 and Ladbroke Grove in 1938	Ladbroke Grove
Portland Road	Renamed in 1917	Great Portland Street
Post Office	Renamed 1937	St Paul's
Putney Bridge & Fulham	Renamed Putney Bridge and Hurlingham in 1902, then Putney Bridge in 1932	Putney Bridge
Queen's Road	Renamed in 1946	Queensway
Shaftesbury Road	Renamed 1888	Ravenscourt Park
Tottenham Court Road	Renamed in 1908	Goodge Street
Walham Green	Renamed in 1952	Fulham Broadway
Westminster Bridge	Renamed 1907	Westminster

7 June 1665

This day, much against my Will, I did in Drury-lane see two or three houses marked with a red cross upon the doors, and 'Lord have mercy upon us' writ there – which was a sad sight to me, being the first of that kind that to my remembrance I ever saw. It put me into an ill conception of myself and my smell, so that I was forced to buy some roll-tobacco to smell and to chew – which took away the apprehension.

3 September 1665

Lords day. Up, and put on my coloured silk suit, very fine, and my new periwig, bought a good while since, but darst not wear it because the plague was in Westminster when I bought it. And it is a wonder what will be the fashion after the plague is done as to periwigs, for nobody will dare to buy any haire for fear of the infection – that it had been cut off the heads of people dead of the plague.

Samuel Pepys, *Diary*

PUB QUIZ

Did you know...

The Mayflower, Rotherhithe Street SE16, is the only pub in England licensed to sell US and UK postage stamps.

Nell of Old Drury, 29 Catherine Street WC2, was once linked to the Theatre Royal, and had an intermission bell in the pub to alert drinkers to the second half, and a tunnel once linked the theatre to the pub.

Two Brewers, 40 Monmouth Street WC2, was once called the Sheep's Head, as the severed head of a sheep was put outside the pub every day.

Lamb and Flag, Rose Street WC2, was once known as the Bucket of Blood because of fistfights held in the upstairs room.

It was in the **Calthorpe Arms**, Gray's Inn Road, where the Brink's-Mat robbery was planned. The first policeman to be killed in London was also killed here.

Chequers, Duke Street SW1, was the first pub to be built after the Great Fire of London.

The Old Red Lion, Holborn WC1, once housed Oliver Cromwell's headless body.

The reason for copies of *The Times* covering the walls of **The Thunderer**, Mount Pleasant Street WC1, is that the paper was once called 'The Thunderer'.

Seven Stars, Carey Street WC2, an early seventeenth century pub is one of the smallest in London.

LONDON CLOCKS

Some of London's more interesting clocks, past and present

The Westminster Clock Tower, otherwise fondly known as Big Ben, which is the name of the 13 1/2 tonne bell that strikes the hour and each quarter.

The mechanical clock at the church of St Dunstan-in-the-West, which overhangs the pavement and has its bell struck on the hour by two apparently indolent giants. The poet John Donne was once the vicar here.

The Apostle Clock, Horniman Museum, which has its own tower, like a miniature Big Ben.

The Fortnum & Mason clock, which rings the hour and the quarters attracting crowds of tourists gazing upwards from Piccadilly.

The Act of Parliament Clock in the George Inn in Borough High Street.

The huge fob watch outside Arthur Saunders watchmaker in Southampton Row.

The Astronomical Clock over the Anne Boleyn Gateway at Hampton Court Palace, made in 1540.

The Zodiacal Clock over the door of Bracken House, Cannon Street, which bears the minutes of the hour, months of the year, the signs of the zodiac and Winston Churchill's scowling face at the centre.

The clock on the tower of the church of St George the Martyr on Borough High Sreet. Of its four faces, the one that faces Bermondsey is never illuminated, allegedly because in the past, the people of that parish failed to make donations to the church.

The clock outside the World's End boutique in Chelsea, which runs backwards at great speed and has 13 hours.

Sadly no longer to be seen... at the Eccentrics Club on Ryder Street, a clock that ran backwards.

FLYING FISH

In February 2004, the Environment Agency was faced with the task of explaining why an Amazonian red-bellied piranha dropped out of the sky and landed on the deck of the Thames Bubbler barge at Halfway Reach in Dagenham, east London. The Agency had to assume that someone had released their pet piranha into the river, which would have died from cold almost immediately. It is thought a seagull then picked up the 10cm-long fish and dropped it, as there were seagull beak marks in its skin. It is not known who was more surprised; the workers on the barge or the seagull.

TRANSPORT STATISTICS

In 2000/01, the last year during which statistics were gathered:

- 1.1 million people entered Central London every day between 7am and 10am
- 84 per cent of these people used public transport
- 79 per cent of people working in central London used public transport to get to work (compared to 14 per cent in the rest of the UK)
- The number of people entering central London to work has increased steadily every year since 1994
- 80 per cent of all vehicles travelling in Greater London each day were cars
- The average number of people per car entering London between 7am and 10am was 1.4
- The average traffic speed in central London was 10mph, compared to 12.3mph in 1979
- The average travel time for people getting to work in central London was 56 minutes, more than twice the national average
- 200,000 Penalty Charge Notices (parking tickets) were issued in Greater London
- The number of Penalty Charge Notices issued in London increased by 25 per cent between 1995 and 2001
- There were over 6.8 million parking spaces in London
- The number of people travelling by bus had increased by 23 per cent since 1994
- The number of people travelling by tube had increased by 21 per cent since 1991
- Each resident of Greater London made 1,000 journeys per year around the city, covering a distance of 5,500 miles
- Residents of inner London used their cars for 50 per cent of their total travel; residents of outer London used their cars for 73 per cent of their total travel
- For door-to-door journeys in central London, a bicycle was the fastest mode of transport. Car journeys took about 50 per cent longer than a bicycle travelling the same route.

LONDON WORDS

Roper's description of the people he calls 'the Necessary Evils'
...the shiny-cheeked merchant bankers from London with eighties striped blue ties and white collars and double-barrelled names and double chins and double-breasted suits, who said 'ears' when they meant 'yes' and 'hice' when they meant 'house' and 'school' when they meant 'Eton'.

John le Carré, *The Night Manager*

Mrs Biggins spent days perfecting the correct approach for getting exactly what she wanted at the Harrods' sale

FISH FACTS

Billingsgate market, now known for its fish, was originally a general market for corn, coal, iron, wine, salt, pottery and miscellaneous goods as well as fish. In 1699 an Act of Parliament made Billingsgate 'a free and open market for all sorts of fish whatsoever' with the exception of the sale of eels. Eels could be sold only by the Dutch fishermen whose boats were moored in the Thames, a privilege granted because they had helped to feed the people of London during the Great Fire. As the market's popularity increased, a permanent building was required, and in 1850 the first Billingsgate Market building was constructed on Lower Thames Street. It soon proved to be inadequate and was demolished in 1873 to make way for a new building, which opened in 1876 and which still stands in Lower Thames Street. Billingsgate is the UK's largest inland fish market and a favourite of London's restaurant chefs. Around 25,000 tonnes of fish and fish products are sold there each year, giving the market an annual turnover of around £200m.

QUOTE UNQUOTE

London is full of women who trust their husbands. One can always recognise them. They look so thoroughly unhappy.
Oscar Wilde, playwright and author

What do Bow Street, Marlborough Street
and Vine Street have in common?
Answer on page 153.

THE ORIGINAL HOOLIGAN

The word 'hooligan' first began to appear in London police-court reports in the summer of 1898. It became instantly popular, and the papers were soon using every derivation they could create, including hooliganism, hooliganesque, hooliganic, and the verb to hooligan. One London newspaper, the *Daily Graphic,* referred in 22 August 1898 to 'the avalanche of brutality which, under the name of "Hooliganism" ...has cast such a dire slur on the social records of South London'.

The Oxford English Dictionary says that the origin of the word is unknown. But in 1899, a man named Clarence Rook claimed in his book, *Hooligan Nights,* that the word derived from a Patrick Hooligan, a small-time bouncer and thief, who lived in the Borough on the south side of the river. Hooligan frequented a pub called the Lamb and Flag with his family and followers, and was imprisoned for murdering a policeman. Similarly, another writer, Earnest Weekley, said in his *Romance of Words* in 1912: 'The original Hooligans were a spirited Irish family of that name whose proceedings enlivened the drab monotony of life in Southwark about fourteen years ago.' His use of 'spirited' and 'enlivened' suggest that he never lived in Southwark himself, nor had he enjoyed having his monotony enlivened by the likes of Hooligan.

THE STREETS ARE PAVED WITH GOLD

The third richest man in the country in 2004 was the Duke of Westminster, who was estimated to be worth £4.63 billion. The Duke, otherwise known as Gerald Cavendish Grosvenor, owns 300 acres of London as well as land in Britain, Europe, Asia and America. In 2003, he was made Knight Companion of the Most Noble Order of the Garter, in the same year that he faced a revolt by his tenants because of high maintenance costs in Eaton Square, from which he had to back down. He also owns an art collection worth around £225 million, which includes a £30 million Van Dyck and a £25 million Stubbs. His enormous wealth is eclipsed only by Roman Abramovich, the Russian businessman and owner of Chelsea football club, and Hans Rausing, the packaging heir. The Queen, who has often topped the list in the past, now sits in 26th position, with a mere £1.05 billion.

THE RIGHT WAY TO DRIVE

The only place in London where one must drive on the right is when turning off the Strand and into the forecourt of the Savoy. The simple explanation is that the turn off the Strand is too sharp for cars to stay on the left, and entering on the right caused fewer scrapes.

IMPRESSIONS OF LONDON

Just some of Canaletto's many paintings of London
'Westminster Bridge from the North on Lord Mayor's Day', *1746*
'Seen through an Arch of Westminster Bridge', *1746–1747*
'Whitehall and the Privy Garden from Richmond House', *1747*
'The Thames and the City of London from Richmond House', *1747*
'Westminster Bridge, London, with the Lord Mayor's Procession on the Thames', *1747*
'Westminster Abbey', *1748*
'Westminster Abbey, with a Procession of Knights of the Bath', *1749*
'The Old Horse Guards and Banqueting Hall, from Saint James' Park', *1749*
'The Old Horse Guards from Saint James' Park', *1749*
'Northumberland House', *1752*
'Greenwich Hospital from the North Bank of the Thames', *c.1753*
'Ranelagh, Interior of the Rotunda', *1754*
'St Paul's Cathedral, London', *1754*

DEATH ON THE UNDERGROUND

The underground became an unofficial hiding-place during the air-raids on London, as citizens took to the only place that felt safe. At first the authorities resisted, but eventually the tubes were run as official shelters. However, this was not without risk, and many deaths ensued, including the following:

Trafalgar Square, 12 October 1940: seven killed when a bomb exploded at the top of the escalator, filling the platforms with earth

Balham, 14 October 1940: 68 killed when a direct hit caused the road to collapse into the tunnel

Bank, 11 January 1941: 56 killed when a bomb exploded in the escalator machine room

Bethnal Green, 3 March 1943: 173 killed when a woman lost her footing at the front of a panicked crowd pouring into the station after an air raid warning. The people behind her piled up on top of each other. Most died from suffocation.

Mornington Crescent Tube station was the inspiration for an absurd game regularly played on the Radio 4 programme *I'm Sorry, I Haven't a Clue*. At first hearing, it seems as if there is a cryptic connection between the names of the tube stations announced by the players. But after a few shows, one begins to suspect that, actually, they're just making it up. Nevertheless, the devoted website, www.isihac.co.uk, goes to great pains to explain the rules and their many variations. In homage to this inspired game, we reproduce some of those here.

The Rules

The website explains, helpfully (and suspiciously) 'As most people know the rules to this game, or can track down the International Mornington Crescent Society rulebook, I will not waste space repeating them here. However, the following are the simplified rules which should be enough to start you playing.'

Rules for Mornington Crescent (simplified)
1. Get to Mornington Crescent.
2. Stop your opponents getting there first.

A few variations

Ancient Ceramic League Ruling
A version possibly played by Josiah Wedgwood himself. Nowadays referred to as Speed Mornington Crescent, this variation has become chiefly the preserve of the showman due both to the strict time limit imposed between moves as well as the suspension of all blind side boundaries. As you can imagine, in the hands of experienced players, it can be breathtaking to watch.

Burlington Original Rules
As defined in Stovold's. All WC postcodes count double, but cannot be followed by a consecutive WC code. Crescents are wild, as rule 42 is, of course, suspended.

Hooper's Mainline Variation
A rather spiteful version with a passing resemblance to Association Croquet. Should one player manage an identical call to that of the previous player, he or she becomes entitled to an extra move. The better the extra move, the further they can force (or Welly) their unfortunate opponent outside the Central Metropolitan Area.

Mortimer's 2nd Amendment
This is a highly specialised version of the game, which, once Parsons Green has been declared, forces play along the Great Western axis, obliging players to sacrifice Seven Sisters in order to prise open their opponent's laterals.

New Standard Livingston Rules
Pedestrianised squares are out of bounds, and any locations subject to a congestion charge incurs a forfeit.

PUB QUIZ

Pubs full of a different kind of spirit...

The Mitre, Craven Terrace W2
Haunted by the ghost of an old coachman who lived in the stables, which were where the cellar bar now is.

Rose & Crown, Old Park Lane W1
Most haunted pub in London, because prisoners heading for Tyburn gallows were often incarcerated in the cellars overnight.

Grenadier, Wilton Row, SW1
Once the officers' mess for the Duke of Wellington's soldiers; the Duke's mounting block used to be kept in a passageway outside. It is haunted by an officer who cheated at cards and was duly flogged, which accidentally led to his death.

John Snow, 39 Broadwick Street W1
Named after a surgeon who helped to quell an outbreak of cholera in the area in the nineteenth century, thanks to his research into waterborne disease.

An image of the village water-pump appears now and then to remind drinkers to stick to beer.

Cheshire Cheese, Little Essex Street WC2
Jacobean and haunted by a very strong ghost who moves the fruit machine.

Crockers, Aberdeen Place NW8
Haunted by its founder, Frank Crocker, distraught by his mistaken impression that trains from Marylebone would stop nearby; the expected customers never materialised.

The Bedford, Bedford Hill SW12
Haunted by Dr James Gully, wrongly convicted in the room upstairs.

Morpeth Arms, Millbank SW1
The cellars are connected to an old tunnel used by prisoners to escape from the Millbank Penitentiary, to avoid being deported to Australia. Said to be haunted by those who didn't make it out.

MARKET DAY

London's best markets

Bermondsey	Friday	*Antiques*
Borough	Fri & Sat	*Food*
Brick Lane	Sun	*Flea market*
Columbia Road	Sun	*Flowers, plants, garden equipment*
Greenwich	Sat & Sun	*Antiques, bric-a-brac, clothes, food*
Northcote Road	Thu–Sat	*Food*
Portobello Road	Sat	*Antiques*
Spitalfields	Mon–Fri, Sun	*Organic food, crafts, gifts; fashion on Sunday*

'Phyllis', also known as 'Rosie' because he wore a rose behind each ear, had been thrown out of the French earlier that day. He darted into the pubs of Soho in order to create a scene. Later, in a very rash moment I gave him half a crown, which meant that forever after if he saw me he made a dash towards me with a cry of joyful recognition: 'Mr Farson, Mr Farson, dear! Give me the price of a drink. Oh, well, give me the kiss of life.' He had a knack of appearing when I was trying to impress someone. His devastating screams and comments were broken off abruptly as he was thrown out, but at least the atmosphere had been enlivened.

Phyllis's real name was Timothy Cotter. Sometimes he'd appear horribly beaten up and people whispered that this had happened when he was arrested. This was not necessarily true, but his only 'fixed address' was Brixton Police Station and it was here that he died after one of his bouts of drunkenness. As he had no relatives and no friends, a pauper's funeral was imminent, but then a wonderful thing happened. The street traders of Berwick Street market took over the responsibility, decorating their stalls with flowers and photographs of Phyllis in order to raise the money to 'send him off' in style. 'The stalls were startling,' Deakin told me, 'like primitive Greek shrines'. Two hundred pounds were raised and Phyllis enjoyed a moment of posthumous approval as the *Daily Mirror* described him as 'an incredibly kind man and well-loved by everybody. His endless kindliness, especially to children, made him a very popular figure.'

Daniel Farson, *Soho in the Fifties*

DEATH, PLAGUE AND OTHER DISASTERS

On the night of 15 October 1987, a severe storm struck southern Britain. In a storm that raged more fiercely than any seen since 1703, 18 people were killed, fifteen million trees were felled, hundreds of thousands of homes were cut off from electricity and several ships were stranded, capsized or blown away. Regular weather forecasts had not warned of a storm as it was thought that the bad weather front would not further North than the English Channel. London and south-east England took the brunt of the storm, as gusts of 70 knots raged for three to four hours, tearing down trees, lifting roofs and displacing bins, benches and other street furniture. Gatwick Airport reported gusts of 86 knots, and 82 knots were recorded at the London Weather Centre. Despite being referred to as a hurricane, the storm cannot be classified as such, as Hurricane Force applies only to a wind of 64 knots or more, sustained over at least 10 minutes. Gusts are not taken into account, even though they cause much of the destruction. In London, the mean wind speed stayed below 44 knots.

FARE ENOUGH

London taxi-drivers are permitted to urinate in public, provided that a member of the police force acts as a witness.

LONDON ROADS

When the powers-that-be were naming some of London's roads, it seems that their minds may have been on more distant locations...

Abyssinia Close, *SW11*
Bangalore Street, *SW15*
Cuba Street, *E14*
Dakota Gardens, *E6*
Edinburgh Road, *W7*
Falkland Avenue, *N11*
Geneva Drive, *SW9*
Hobart Close, *N20*
Iceland Road, *E3*
Jersey Road, *E11*
Khyber Road, *SW11*
Lindisfarne Road, *SW20*
Madeira Road, *N13*
North Pole Road, *W10*
Ontario Street, *SE1*
Perth Avenue, *NW9*
Quebec Way, *SE16*
Rawalpindi House, *E16*
South Africa Road, *W12*
Toronto Road, *E11*
Ulster Terrace, *NW1*
Virginia Street, *E1*
Wales Close, *SE15*
Yukon Road, *SW12*
Zealand Road, *E3*

LONGEST-SERVING COMMITTEE MEMBER

Jeremy Bentham was an eighteenth-century philosopher whose macabre sense of humour has left London with a peculiar legacy. He left a large sum of money to University College on condition that when he died, his skeleton would continue to attend the annual general meeting. His skeleton is duly wheeled along to the AGM each year, preserved in a mahogany case, seated in a chair and holding his favourite walking stick. Bentham is also taken to the weekly meeting of the board of governors, where he is recorded as present but is not allowed to vote.

LONDON – THE EARLY YEARS

A beginner's guide to London's early history

55 BC	Julius Caesar invades Britain
43	Claudius establishes London and builds the first bridge over the Thames
60	Boadicea attacks and burns London to the ground
200	City wall built
410	Roman troops begin to leave London
604	King Ethelbert builds the first St Paul's Cathedral
834	The Vikings invade
884	Alfred the Great takes power
1014	Olaf invades London and pulls down London Bridge
1042	Edward the Confessor becomes king
1065	Westminster Abbey completed
1066	William I is crowned king in the Abbey
1086	Domesday Book is completed
1176	Work begins on the first stone London Bridge – the only bridge across the Thames until 1750
1189	Henry Fitzailwyn becomes the first mayor of London
1197	Richard I sells control of the River Thames to the Corporation of London
1240	First Parliament sits at Westminster
1348	Black Death cuts the population by half
1381	Peasants' Revolt
1397	Richard Whittington becomes mayor

SOUNDS FAMILIAR

The Festival of Britain may ring a few bells with today's London residents. It was held on derelict land near Waterloo. Most of it was held within the Dome of Discovery, surrounded by pavilions dedicated to educational, scientific exhibitions. There was also the Skylon, a cigar-shaped – perhaps gherkin-shaped? – tower. Evelyn Waugh mentioned 'Monstrous constructions appeared on the south bank of the Thames', and Keith Waterhouse harrumphed that the whole thing was 'a monument to British tat; escalators which didn't work, elegant glass entrance halls stuck over with scrawled notices reading "Use other door"...'

QUOTE UNQUOTE

A broken heart is a very pleasant complaint for a man in London if he has a comfortable income.
George Bernard Shaw, author and playwright

114 *Number, in 100,000s, of car parking spaces available at London stations*

I made myself sob less, and persuaded myself to be quiet by saying very often, 'Esther, now you really must! This will not do!' I cheered myself up pretty well at last, though I am afraid I was longer about it than I ought to have been; and when I had cooled my eyes with lavender water, it was time to watch for London.

I was quite persuaded that we were there, when we were ten miles off; and when we really were there, that we should never get there. However, when we began to jolt upon a stone pavement, and particularly when every other conveyance seemed to be running into us, and we seemed to be running into every other conveyance, I began to believe that we really were approaching the end of our journey. Very soon afterwards, we stopped.

A young gentleman who had inked himself by accident, addressed me from the pavement, and said, 'I am from Kenge and Carboy's, miss, of Lincoln's Inn.'

'If you please, sir,' said I.

He was very obliging; and as he handed me into a fly, after super-intending the removal of my boxes, I asked him whether there was a great fire anywhere? For the streets were so full of dense brown smoke that scarcely anything was to be seen.

'O dear no, miss,' he said. 'This is a London particular.'

I had never heard of such a thing.

'A fog, miss,' said the young gentleman.

'O indeed!' said I.

We drove slowly through the dirtiest and darkest streets that ever were seen in the world (I thought) and in such a distracting state of confusion that I wondered how the people kept their senses...

Charles Dickens, *Bleak House*

OUT OF TOWN

Not every famous London resident had a posh Mayfair address...
- Sir Ernest Henry Shackleton lived at 12 Westwood Hill SE26
- Sir Noel Coward lived at 131 Waldegrave Road, Teddington
- William Heath-Robinson lived at 75 Moss Lane, Pinner
- Samuel Taylor Coleridge lived in Dagnall Park, South Norwood, SE25
- William Bligh lived at 100 Lambeth Road, Lambeth, SE1
- John Logie Baird lived at 3 Crescent Wood Road, Sydenham, SE26
- Joseph Chamberlain lived in Camberwell Grove, Camberwell, SE5

CAPITAL CONUNDRUMS

What is unusual about the waiters at Pratt's?
Answer on page 153.

Outstanding London cricket matches through the years...

18–21 August 1994, The Oval: England v South Africa, third Test Match
West Indian bowler Devon Malcolm devastates South Africa by taking 9 for 57. Spectators claim that his performance improved after he took a blow to his helmet earlier in the Test.

2–7 July 1981, Lord's: England v Australia, second Test Match
Ian Botham scores a duck twice in his last match as captain, and leaves the field to complete silence from the crowd. (But he redeemed himself at the next Test match in Headingley, in a superb comeback for England.)

22–26 June 1972, Lord's: England v Australia, second Test Match
Aussie bowler Bob Massie marks his first Test Match by taking 8 for 84 in the first innings and 8 for 53 in his second.

15–19 August 1953, The Oval: England v Australia, fifth Test Match
England regain the Ashes for the first time in 20 years. It is also the first time since 1926 that England has beaten Australia at home.

24-29 June 1950, Lord's: England v West Indies, second Test Match
The West Indies achieve their first win in England. The delighted supporters stage an impromptu celebration march from Lord's to central London.

21–25 June 1947, Lord's: England v South Africa, second Test Match
In an unbeaten third-wicket partnership, Denis Compton and Bill Edrich put on 370 runs

21–24 August 1938, The Oval: England v Australia, fifth Test Match
Len Hutton creates a new world record of 364 runs, and England declare at 903 for 7. Australia lose by an innings and 579 runs.

27 June–1 July 1930, at Lord's: England v Australia, second Test Match
Donald Bradman scores 254 in his first Test Match at Lord's

28–29 August 1882, The Oval: The 'Ashes' Test
England lose to Australia by just seven runs, despite needing only 85 in their second innings to win. The next day, the *Sporting Times* carried the now-famous obituary: 'In Affectionate Remembrance of ENGLISH CRICKET, which died at the Oval on 29th August 1882. Deeply lamented by a large circle of Sorrowing Friends and Acquaintances, RIP. NB – The body will be cremated and the Ashes taken to Australia.' This began the tradition of referring to the Test Matches between the two countries as The Ashes.

OLD PICTURE, NEW CAPTION

*A traffic warden patiently explains the concept of a
red route to some bemused tourists*

QUOTE UNQUOTE

Her mystery was as thick as a London fog.
Tallulah Bankhead, actress, on Greta Garbo

BRING IN THE FLYING SQUAD

Robberies and attempted robberies at Heathrow airport

November 1983	Gold bars and diamonds worth £26 million stolen. The thieves were apprehended and jailed for 25 years
December 1991	Police prevent an attempt to kidnap an airline worker in order to gain access to a warehouse containing £26 million worth of goods
August 1994	£850,000 in used banknotes stolen by thieves who used tear gas to overcome the unfortunate courier
January 2000	A man hid in the hold of flight to Madrid in order to steal £1.5 million in Spanish currency. He was arrested on the return flight
February 2002	£4.57 million in foreign currency stolen from a BA security van
February 2002	26,000 mobile phones stolen from a Samsung warehouse
March 2002	Police arrest 12 people attempting to hijack a van carrying £1.8 million
May 2004	100 police overpower eight armed robbers attempting to steal £40 million in gold bullion and £40 million in cash from a warehouse

Number, in thousands, of people who slept in the Underground on 117
27 September 1940

ART BY THE YARD

Sir James Thornhill who painted the exceptionally beautiful interior of the Painted Hall at the Royal Naval College in Greenwich between 1707 and 1726, was paid £3 per square yard for the ceiling and £1 per square yard for the walls.

BRITISH LIBRARY

Facts and figures about the British Library that will please the librarian in all of us

- It receives a copy of every publication produced in the UK and Ireland
- The collection includes 150 million items, in most known languages, dating from 300 BC to the present day
- Three million new items are incorporated every year
- It holds manuscripts, maps, newspapers, magazines, prints and drawings, music scores, and patents
- The Sound Archive keeps sound recordings from nineteenth-century cylinders to the latest CD, DVD and minidisc recordings
- The collection includes 310,000 manuscript volumes, from Jane Austen to the Beatles
- It houses eight million stamps and other philatelic items
- It holds 49.5 million patents
- It holds over four million maps
- It holds over 260,000 journal titles
- The shelf space grows by 12 kilometres every year
- A person inspecting five items a day would take 80,000 years to see the whole of the collection
- It carries out six million searches a year generated by the online catalogue
- Around half a million people visit the reading rooms each year
- Its key possessions include the Magna Carta, the Lindisfarne Gospels, the first dated printed book, *The Diamond Sutra*, Leonardo da Vinci's Notebook, the first edition of *The Times* from 18 March 1788 and the recording of Nelson Mandela's trial speech
- The new building at St Pancras was the largest public building constructed in the UK in the twentieth century, and required 10 million bricks and 180,000 tonnes of concrete

SMOKIN'!

The all-American Marlboro brand of cigarettes was named after the Philip Morris factory, which in 1902 was situated on Marlborough Street.

PUB QUIZ

Did you know...

Marquis of Granby, Chandos Place WC2
The Bow Street Runners caught Claude Duval in here, who was hanged for highway robbery

I Am The Only Running Footman, Charles Street W1
'Running footmen' ran ahead of carriages to clear the way and pay tolls.

French House, Dean Street W1
The London centre for the Free French movement during World War Two. De Gaulle drank here, as well as Brendan Behan and Dylan Thomas.

Silver Cross, Whitehall SW1
Thirteenth century building with wagon-vaulted ceiling. Licensed as a brothel by Charles I.

Ye Olde Cheshire Cheese, Fleet Street EC4
Customers included Samuel Johnson, Alexander Pope, Voltaire and Charles Dickens (who mentions it in his *A Tale of Two Cities*). The fourteenth century crypt of Whitefriars monastery is still intact below the cellar bar.

George Inn, Borough High Street, SE1
London's only intact galleried coaching inn. Charles Dickens drank here.

The Flask, Highgate West Hill N6
Built in 1663. Dick Turpin hid in the cellars once. Hogarth drew in the bar, and Karl Marx was a regular.

Dover Castle, Weymouth Mews W1
Strip mirrors in the ceiling were installed so that coachmen pausing for refreshment could see when their employers had finished their drink and get back to the coach before them

Queen's Head, Brook Green W6
Dick Turpin once hid here from his pursuers.

A NICE SPOT FOR A PICNIC

On 23 October 1843, 14 people ate a meal on the platform at the top of Nelson's Column, just before the statue of Nelson was erected.

When in 1660 Charles II regained the throne taken from his father, the immorality of his court caused many to predict that a terrible judgment would be visited upon him, and the date often mentioned was 1666, as 666 was the devil's number.

In September 1666, the city was tinder-dry after a long drought, and the fire that famously started at a baker's in Pudding Lane on 1 September took hold quickly and raged furiously through the streets. The ineffectual Mayor, Sir Thomas Bludworth, not only underestimated the seriousness of the fire – 'A woman could piss it out,' he claimed before returning to bed – but also would not authorise the pulling down of four houses to act as a firebreak, as he was worried about who would pay for the rebuilding. His decision, or lack of it, cost London dearly. At one point 100 houses an hour were being consumed by fire.

It was, in fact, Samuel Pepys who went to the king and insisted that he intervene and order the mayor to create a firebreak. Charles had always enjoyed fighting the frequent fires that took hold in his city, and he gave the order. But the fire burned on. People scattered from the city with their belongings in carts, and suspected arsonists were beaten in the streets. The fire burned from Saturday night until Wednesday, until the wind finally dropped and the firefighters were able to finally bring it under control, bit by bit, just before it reached the Tower of London, with its stores of gunpowder. Around 436 acres of London were destroyed and only 75 acres saved. One in three houses burned down, as well as many important and historic buildings, such as the Royal Exchange and Newgate Prison. The city lost 87 churches, 44 livery halls and 13,200 houses. And while 70,000 people were made homeless, the most astonishing statistic of the fire was the death toll – only six people perished. Another was that by 11 September, Christopher Wren had already submitted plans for rebuilding the city. And finally, a Frenchman named Robert Hubert claimed to have pushed fireballs through the window of the bakery and was held responsible for starting the fire. No one believed he was guilty, but he was hanged anyway.

LONDON WORDS

Oh London is a fine town
A very famous city
Where the streets are paved with gold,
And all the maidens pretty.
George Colman the Younger, *The Heir at Law, Act I*

London's earliest Tube stations are over 150 years old, though some opened as overland stations first. The dates given here are when the station opened on its present site; many were built earlier, but moved.

Barbican	*23 December 1865*
Barkin	*13 April 1854*
Bromley by Bow	*31 March 1858, first used by Tube trains in June 1902*
Buckhurst Hill	*22 August 1856, first used by Tube trains in November 1948*
Debden	*24 April 1865, first used by Tube trains in September 1949*
East Ham	*31 March 1858, first used by Tube trains in June 1902*
Edgware Road	*10 January 1863*
Epping	*24 April 1865, first used by Tube trains in September 1949*
Euston Square	*10 January 1863*
Farringdon	*10 January 1863*
Great Portland Street	*10 January 1863*
Hammersmith & City	*13 June 1864*
Harrow & Wealdstone	*20 July 1837, first used by Tube trains in April 1917*
Kensington Olympia	*27 May 1844 (since relocated)*
King's Cross	*10 January 1863*
Ladbroke Grove	*13 June 1864*
Leyton	*22 August 1856, first used by Tube trains in May 1947*
Leytonstone	*22 August 1856, first used by Tube trains in May 1947*
Loughton	*24 April 1865 (opened on a different site on 22 August 1856)*
Moorgate	*23 December 1865*
Plaistow	*31 March 1858, first used by Tube trains in June 1902*
Richmond	*27 July 1846, first used by Tube trains in June 1877*
Shepherd's Bush	*13 June 1864 (Hammersmith & City)*
Snaresbrook	*22 August 1856*
South Woodford	*22 August 1856*
Theydon Bois	*24 April 1865*
Wembley	*1842, first used by Tube trains April 1917*
Woodford	*22 August 1856, first used by Tube trains in December 1947*

EXTREME STATISTICS

- London has the highest population of any European city.
- London has the busiest airport in Europe: Heathrow handles around 53 million passengers a year.
- London has the most congested ring-road in Europe, the M25
- Oxford Street is the busiest shopping street in Europe, with 200 million visitors a year and a total turnover of £5 billion.
- London has the most street markets of any city in the western world.
- There are more billionaires in London than there are in any other world city.
- London was the first city in the world after the Middle Ages where the population exceeded 1 million. In 1811, there were 1,009,546 people in the city. It remained the largest city in the world until 1957, when it was overtaken by Tokyo.
- London has the sixth largest library in the world, which is the British Library. It was founded in 1753 and contains 15 million books.
- London has the largest local authority archives in the UK.
- London holds the oldest dedicated collection of clocks and watches in the world, at the Guildhall Library.
- London has the longest escalator in western Europe at Angel Underground Station, which consists of 318 steps.
- London has the longest underground rail network in the world, which comprises a total length of 392 kilometres of track.
- London has the fourth longest underground tunnel in the world, the Northern Line from East Finchley to Morden. It was completed in 1939 and measures 27.8 kilometres in length.

QUOTE UNQUOTE

On my regular walk to the Central Line tube station I compose denunciations to the Hammersmith and Fulham Council on the squalid shambles that is Shepherd's Bush.
Douglas Hurd, former Foreign Secretary, complaining to the *Evening Standard* in 2004 about the litter-strewn state of his local streets

IT'S MY CLUB AND I'LL SMOKE IF I WANT TO

The now-defunct Marlborough Club was established by the future Edward VII, when he was sent to the smoking room in White's in order to enjoy a cigar. In a fit of pique, he set up his own club, where he could smoke wherever and whenever he wanted.

A few lesser-known facts about the permanent inhabitants of Westminster Abbey

Clement Attlee (1883–1967)
Prime Minister
Was also a published poet

William Congreve (1670–1729)
playwright
His monument was paid for by his mistress, the second Duchess of Marlborough, with some of the money that he left her

Oliver Cromwell (1599–1658)
His body was exhumed in 1661 by Charles II when the king was restored to the throne. His body was symbolically hanged, then decapitated and his head displayed on a pole outside Westminster Hall by the vengeful king

George Frederick Handel (1685–1759) *composer*
Who asked in his will to be buried in the Abbey, which was unusually presumptuous

David Livingstone (1813–1873)
missionary and traveller
Most rather than all of him is buried here – his internal organs are buried in an Arabian village

Ben Jonson (1572/3–1637) *poet*
The only person to be buried here standing up, allegedly because he was too poor to afford more space

Edward VI, (1537–1553)
The first sovereign to be interred using the burial service from his own prayer book, The Book of Common Prayer

Edward Montagu (1661–1715)
Edward, First Earl of Sandwich. Shipwrecked, drowned and his body nibbled by porpoises

Sir Clowdisley Shovel (1650–1707) *admiral*
Shipwrecked then killed by a fisherwoman for his emerald ring

Elizabeth Russell (1575–1601)
Godchild of Elizabeth I. The first effigy in the Abbey to be depicted sitting up

Frederick Louis (1707–1751)
Son of George II, killed by a tennis ball

Samuel Johnson (1709–1784)
writer and lexicographer
Died in the night after cutting open his own leg to relieve swelling

Thomas Parr (1483–1635)
died aged 152 years and nine months; he lived though the reign of 10 monarchs and was buried here on the orders of King Charles I

Laurence Olivier (1907–1989)
actor
Person most recently buried in the Abbey

Carruthers demonstrated the strength of his feelings about the pigeons in Trafalgar Square

DEATH, PLAGUES AND OTHER DISASTERS

London's worst Tube crash took place in February 1975 at Moorgate station. The 8.37am from Drayton Park overshot the platform and crashed at 30mph into a dead-end tunnel at 8.46am. The driver and 42 passengers were killed, and 74 were injured. The rescue teams were hampered by the intense heat generated underground, and the last survivor was not brought out until 10pm. An emergency operating area was erected on the platform and was attended by doctors and nurses from local hospitals. The cause of the crash was a mystery; the driver was in good health with an unblemished record and had not taken drugs or alcohol. But the guard said that he felt the train speed up as it entered the station, and investigations showed that the brakes were never applied and the driver did not appear to have put his hands up to shield himself before the impact. There appeared to be nothing wrong with the train, signals or track. The cause has never been established.

LONDON WORDS

Nowhere in the streets of London may one escape the sight of abject poverty, while five minutes' walk from almost any point will bring one to a slum; but the region my hansom was now penetrating was one unending slum. The streets were filled with a new and different race of people, short of stature, and of wretched or beer-sodden appearance. We rolled along through miles of bricks and squalor, and from each cross street and alley flashed long vistas of bricks and misery. Here and there lurched a drunken man or woman, and the air was obscene with sounds of jangling and squabbling. At a market, tottery old men and women were searching in the garbage thrown in the mud for rotten potatoes, beans, and vegetables, while little children clustered like flies around a festering mass of fruit, thrusting their arms to the shoulders into the liquid corruption, and drawing forth morsels, but partially decayed, which they devoured on the spot.

Not a hansom did I meet with in all my drive, while mine was like an apparition from another and better world, the way the children ran after it and alongside. And as far as I could see were the solid walls of brick, the slimy pavements, and the screaming streets; and for the first time in my life the fear of the crowd smote me. It was like the fear of the sea; and the miserable multitudes, street upon street, seemed so many waves of a vast and malodorous sea, lapping about me and threatening to well up and over me.

'Stepney, sir; Stepney Station,' the cabby called down.

I looked about. It was really a railroad station, and he had driven desperately to it as the one familiar spot he had ever heard of in all that wilderness.

'Well?' I said.

He spluttered unintelligibly, shook his head, and looked very miserable. 'I'm a strynger 'ere,' he managed to articulate. 'An' if yer don't want Stepney Station, I'm blessed if I know wotcher do want.'

Jack London, *The People of the Abyss*

LONDON FIRSTS

- Nicholas Barbon formed London's first fire brigade in 1680.
- Alexander Waugh, brother of Evelyn, claimed to have held the first cocktail party in Britain in 1924. Only one guest turned up.
- In 1880 the Telephone Company Ltd issued the first known phone directory. It listed 250 names connected to three London exchanges.
- In 1829 the UK's first scheduled bus service ran between Bank and Marylebone Road. The bus was horse-drawn.
- The UK's first policewomen were Mary Allen and Margaret Dawson, who trod their beat in London in 1914.

CAPITAL CONUNDRUMS

Which Londonite am I?   GSLIVT   *Answer on page 153.*
                          E

LONDON ON LOCATION

Some classic London films

The Lodger (1927) • *The Man Who Knew Too Much (1934)*
Sabotage (1936) • *Stagefright (1950)*
Oliver Twist (1948) • *The Blue Lamp (1949)*
Passport to Pimlico (1949) • *The Ladykillers (1955)*
The Pumpkin Eater (1964) • *Mary Poppins (1964)*
Blow-Up (1966) • *Alfie (1966)* • *Georgy Girl (1966)*
To Sir with Love (1966) • *Performance (1969)*
A Clockwork Orange (1971) • *Frenzy (1972)*
The Long Good Friday (1979)
An American Werewolf in London (1981)
Dance with a Stranger (1984) • *Mona Lisa (1985)*
My Beautiful Laundrette (1985) • *Absolute Beginners (1986)*
Withnail and I (1987) • *A Fish Called Wanda (1988)*
The Madness of King George (1994)
Shakespeare in Love (1998)
Lock, Stock and Two Smoking Barrels (1998)
Bridget Jones's Diary (2001)

THREE HUNDRED AND FIFTY YEARS LATER...

In 1654, Oliver Cromwell began the process of granting livery status to London cab drivers, by appointing the Court of Aldermen to regulate the city's first licensed carriages. But as civil unrest grew, the process was never completed, and the cab drivers' livery status remained in limbo until the 1980s. Then a cab driver called Phil Warren discovered this little known oversight and began to write about it, which encouraged a group of taxi drivers to finish what Cromwell had started by beginning the long process of becoming a fully fledged Livery company. In 1990, cab drivers were granted Fellowship status by the City of London, and seven years later – the required waiting time – they were declared a Company and were able to apply for full Worshipful status. This was finally granted in 2004, making cab drivers the 104th livery company in London – the Worshipful Company of Hackney Cab Drivers. One hopes the meter wasn't running all that time.

THE STORY OF THE GLOBE

Towards the end of the last century, the director Sam Wanamaker made it his personal duty to rebuild the Globe Theatre, which was first built in 1599. As a building, its career had been short; partially burned down in 1613 thanks to a cannon that was misfired from the balcony, it was closed for ever in 1642 by the Puritans.

The new Globe duly opened in 1997, although Wanamaker died before he could see his achievement realised. The rebuilt Globe, which sits about 200 yards from its original site, holds only 1,700 people, partly due to fire regulations and partly because people are somewhat bigger these days. The new Globe is the first building with a thatched roof to be built in London since the Great Fire of 1666, an exception to the city's building regulations that was allowed only because the thatching reed was covered with fire retardant substance, bedded on fireboards and fitted with discreet sprinklers. Special fire tests on the building materials revealed that the Globe's walls (made of green oak beams and lime plaster) are capable of withstanding heat of around 1000 degrees for two hours 53 minutes and 37 seconds before actually catching fire.

CAN YOU HEAR ME AT THE BACK?

Famous names who have lectured at Speaker's Corner

Tony Benn, *Labour MP*

Frederick Engels, *co-author of* The Communist Manifesto

Marcus Garvey, *black nationalist leader*

Reverend Jesse Jackson, *US congressman*

(on a stage near Speakers Corner at the 2003 Stop the War March)

C.L.R. James, *philosopher, historian, writer, politician and Marxist*

Vladimir Lenin, *Marxist and leader of the 1917 Russian revolution*

Karl Marx, *revolutionary communist and co-author of* The Communist Manifesto

William Morris, *artist, designer and socialist*

George Orwell, *writer*

Christabel Pankhurst, *suffragette*

Ben Tillet, *socialist*

WALKING TO WORK

In 1327, Edward III granted market rights to the City of London in a charter that prohibited the setting up of rival markets within 6.6 miles of the City. This very specific distance was the furthest a person could be expected to walk to market, sell his produce and return in a day.

Cost, in thousands of pounds, of building the Greenwich Foot Tunnel 127
under the Thames in 1902

*In London, love and scandal are considered
the best sweeteners of tea.*
John Osborne, playwright

LONDON LEGENDS

Dick Whittington

Dick Whittington, pantomime legend, was the son of Sir William Whittington, a Gloucestershire landowner. After his father died in 1358, Dick travelled to London to enrol with the Mercers' Company as an apprentice. Whittington proved to be very astute at trading valuable imported silks and velvets as worn by the court and had become a very rich man by the time he was 40. In 1393 he was made a City alderman, and in 1397 he was appointed by the king to the position of Lord Mayor, as the incumbent had died in office. Whittington was then elected Mayor at the next election, and twice more in his lifetime, effectively making him Lord Mayor four times. He became an important benefactor, creating a library at Greyfriars' Monastery, a refuge for unmarried mothers at St Thomas's Hospital, a large public lavatory and a new church, St Michael Paternoster.

He also made bequests that enabled building work to continue after his death, including the rebuilding of Newgate Gaol, a library at Guildhall, and a college for priests and an almshouse, known as Whittington College, which stood next to St Michael's Church. Although the church burned down in 1666, the college still exists, having moved to Highgate in 1821 and then to West Sussex in 1965, and it is still run by the Mercers' Company with income from the City estate that Whittington left for the purpose. Other grants to medical establishments were made as recently as 1986, making Whittington's influence one of the most long-lasting in London. The pantomime fable involving black cats, city bells and affairs with the boss's daughter was first seen in print in 1605, but none of the details, except the making of his fortune, is thought to be true.

THE MUSICAL DICTATOR

Italian dictator Benito Mussolini so enjoyed the song 'The Lambeth Walk' from the 1937 musical *Me and My Girl* that he engaged a London girl to travel to Italy to teach it to him.

LONDON FARMS

Coram's Fields
Guildford St, WC1
Rabbits, guinea pigs,
budgies and sheep

Hackney City Farm
Goldsmith's Row, E2
Pigs, chickens, sheep, geese,
rabbits, guinea pigs, ducks,
turkeys and cows

Kentish Town City Farm
Grafton Road NW5
Horses, cows, sheep, pigs,
rabbits, goats, chickens

Mudchute Park Farm
Pier Street E14
Horses, goats, cows, sheep,
llamas, pigs, dogs, chickens,
ducks and geese

Spitalfields Farm
Weaver Street E1
Cows, donkeys, pigs, sheep,
goats, dogs, chickens, ducks,
geese, rats, mice, rabbits, guinea
pigs, ferrets and cats

Stepping Stones Farm
Stepney Way E1
Donkeys, goats, pigs, rabbits,
guinea pigs, chickens, ferrets,
geese, cats and dogs

Freightliners Farm
Sheringham Road, N7
Ducks, geese, turkeys, guinea
fowl, quail, pigeons, doves,
rabbits, guinea pigs, chinchillas,
chipmunks and unusual breeds of
chicken, including the Aracuana
chicken, which lays green eggs

LONDON WORDS

[My grandchildren and I] were then driven to the Zoological Gardens, a place which I often like to visit (keeping away from the larger beasts, such as the bears, who I often fancy may jump from their poles upon certain unoffending Christians; and the howling tigers and lions, who are continually biting the keepers' heads off), and where I like to look at the monkeys in the cages (the little rascals!) and the birds of various plumage.

Fancy my feelings, Sir, when I saw in these gardens – in these gardens frequented by nursery-maids, mothers, and children – an immense brute of an elephant, about a hundred feet high, rushing about with a wretched little child on his back, and a single man vainly endeavouring to keep him back! I uttered a shriek; I called my dear children round about me. And I am not ashamed to confess it, Sir, I ran. I ran for refuge into a building hard by, where I saw – ah, Sir, I saw an immense boa constrictor swallowing a live rabbit – swallowing a live rabbit, Sir, and looking as if he would have swallowed one of my little boys afterwards. Good heavens! Sir, do we live in a Christian country, and are parents and children to be subjected to sights like these?

WM Thackeray, *Contributions to Punch*

The number of men executed south of Kensington between 1678 and 1799 129

In 1780, a builder discovered to his surprise a series of underground caverns in Blackheath, which had been excavated from chalk and were connected by passages, descending to a depth of 160 feet. The caverns were named 'Jack Cade's Caverns' after the rebel leader who had amassed a civil army on Blackheath in 1450, although it is not suggested that he constructed or used them. One theory is that the caverns dated back to the fifth century, when they were used by frightened locals to hide from the invading Saxons and Danes after the withdrawal of the Romans. The other is that they were created when chalk was excavated in large quantities to help with the construction of St Paul's Cathedral.

When they were rediscovered in 1780, a flight of steps was built to lead down into them, and they became first a local point of interest, and, in the nineteenth century, a popular venue for night-time entertainment. The public could take a torchlight tour of the caves for 4d or 6d; and when a bar, chandelier and ventilation system were installed, drinking parties and balls were held there, the only disadvantage being that if the lights went out (as they often did), panic tended to spoil the party. They were eventually sealed up in 1854. The local council attempted to reopen them in 1906 without success, but they tried again in 1938, with the intention of turning them into air-raid shelters. Graffiti and other mementoes of its former life were found, including the brass ring that had held the chandelier, and the council created new ventilation shafts and extra support; however, the caves were never used as shelters as they were not considered to be safe. Indeed, subsidence in the area has proved a problem; in the worst incident in Kidbrooke in 1798, a hole so large opened up in the ground that it swallowed up a horse.

MR PARROT AND THE FOUR-MINUTE DASH

While most people think that Roger Bannister ran the first four-minute mile in Oxford in 1954, an historian called Peter Radford thinks differently. He claimed, in 2004, that the record was broken 184 years earlier in London. According to Radford's research, in 1770, a market trader named James Parrot ran a mile from Charterhouse Wall in Goswell Road and then the length of Old Street in under four minutes, to settle a bet – the equivalent of £1,380 in today's money. Radford's theory has upset the scientists, who claim that human athletic abilities improve over the centuries, and that no one could have run that fast in the eighteenth century, especially without the benefit of modern training techniques. But perhaps they overlook the motivational effects of a large pile of cash at the finishing post.

QUOTE UNQUOTE

*If people don't like Marxism, they should
blame the British Museum.*
Mikhail Gorbachev, former leader of the Soviet Union

DESIGNING WOMEN

A list of patented inventions exhibited by London women at an exhibition in Chicago in 1883

Portable household washing copper: *Miss Mary Brown, Clapham*
Music folio and stand: *Mrs Bewicke Calverley, St James's Park*
Appliance for lifting hot plates: *Mrs F Tenison, Uxbridge Road*
Clothes washer: *Mrs S Mackie, Chancery Lane*
Sanitary sink basket: *Miss I Peckover, Bloomsbury*
Knee music stand: *Miss M Stephenson*
Specimen of painting on textiles: *Miss D Turck, St George's Square*
Improved ear trumpet: *Mrs M Phillipps, Kilburn*

However, none were quite so ingenious as another member of their group, a Miss Barron from East Moseley, who invented a collapsible noiseless coal-scuttle as well as a combined dress-stand and fire escape made of basketwork.

CAPITAL CONUNDRUMS

Why was the Royal Exchange exit of Bank tube station so convenient?
Answer on page 153.

LONDON WORDS

'The Signora had no business to do it,' said Miss Bartlett, 'no business at all. She promised us south rooms with a view close together, instead of which here are north rooms, looking into a courtyard, and a long way apart. Oh, Lucy!'

'And a Cockney, besides!' said Lucy, who had been further saddened by the Signora's unexpected accent. 'It might be London.' She looked at the two rows of English people who were sitting at the table; at the row of white bottles of water and red bottles of wine that ran between the English people; at the portraits of the late Queen and the late Poet Laureate that hung behind the English people, heavily framed; at the notice of the English church (Rev. Cuthbert Eager, M. A. Oxon.), that was the only other decoration of the wall. 'Charlotte, don't you feel, too, that we might be in London? I can hardly believe that all kinds of other things are just outside. I suppose it is one's being so tired.'

EM Forster, *A Room with a View*

Films shot in and around Covent Garden:

- *The Red Shoes* (1948): the Royal Opera House provides the backdrop for the opening scenes.
- *Modesty Blaise* (1966): the heroine is lured out of retirement while watching a performance at the Royal Opera House.
- Hitchcock's *Frenzy* (1972) was shot in the old Covent Garden, when it was still an open market selling flowers, fruit and vegetables.
- *Scenes from Travels with my Aunt* (1972) were shot in the Lamb and Flag pub in Rose Street, and the aunt's flat was shot above the Salisbury pub in St Martin's Lane.
- In *Four Weddings and a Funeral* (1994), Andie MacDowell and Hugh Grant swop ex-lover statistics in the Dome restaurant in Wellington Street.
- The climactic scene in *Notting Hill* (1999) takes place in the Savoy Hotel, as Hugh Grant gatecrashes the press conference.
- In *Billy Elliott* (2000), his father and brother travel to London to see him perform, and arrive late at the Theatre Royal, Drury Lane.
- Somerset House has appeared in numerous films, and not always as itself; Edward Fox acquired a false birth certificate there in *The Day of the Jackal* (1973); in *Goldeneye* (1995) it doubled for St Petersburg, and became MI6 headquarters in *Tomorrow Never Dies* (1997). It became a turn-of-the-century New York building in *Sleepy Hollow* (1999), the exterior of Oscar Wilde's apartment in *Wilde* (1998) and a Russian building attacked by Bolsheviks in *Reds* (1981). It also played bit parts in *The Secret Agent* (1995), *Sense and Sensibility* (1995) and *Black Beauty* (1994).
- The one film that should have been set in Covent Garden – *My Fair Lady* – where Eliza Doolittle sold her flowers, was shot in a studio.

LONDON FACTS AND FIGURES

London has:
- A population of 7.2 million, the largest city in the UK
- 143 parks and gardens
- 233 nightclubs
- 26 street markets
- 267 tube stations
- 3,800 pubs, comprising 9% of Britain's public houses
- 6,128 licensed restaurants
- Almost 21,000 licensed taxis
- About 11,450,000 visitors each year
- About 300 spoken languages

*It was a Sunday afternoon, wet and cheerless; and a duller spectacle
this earth of ours has not to show than a rainy Sunday in London.*
Thomas de Quincey, writer,
recalling the day when he first took opium

OLD PICTURE, NEW CAPTION

*No matter the weather, as long as Cliff Richard was in the
stands, the players played on.*

HERE BE CRIMINALS

In 1903, Charles Booth produced an intricately coloured map of
London, indicating the living conditions of its residents, which was
dubbed the 'Poverty Map'. It offered the following categories to
describe each area's inhabitants:
• Upper-middle and Upper classes. Wealthy.
• Middle-class. Well-to-do.
• Fairly comfortable. Good ordinary earnings.
• Mixed. Some comfortable, others poor.
• Poor. 18s to 21s a week for a moderate family
• Very poor, casual. Chronic want.
• Lowest class. Vicious, semi-criminal
The full map can be seen at http://booth.lse.ac.uk.

Madame Tussaud

Marie Grosholz was born in Strasbourg in 1761 and learned the art of wax modelling from her mother's employer, Dr Philippe Curtius. The first likeness she made, in 1777, was of Voltaire. In 1780, she was appointed art tutor to King Louis XVI's sister, and went to live at the royal court in Versailles. When the French Revolution broke out, she was obliged to mould heads of some of the victims of the guillotine, some of whom had been her friends at court. In 1794 she inherited Curtius's collection of figures, and a year later married François Tussaud. As Madame Tussaud, she took her collection of figures to England in 1802, where she opened her first exhibition at the Lyceum Theatre in London. It was an instant success, and the show toured England and Scotland for 33 years. Marie survived a shipwreck in the Irish Sea and a fire during the Bristol Riots of 1831, and still managed to create new figures to add to the show as she travelled, finally settling at premises in Baker Street in 1835. After her death in 1850, the exhibition remained at Baker Street until 1884, when her grandsons moved it to its present site in Marylebone Road. The entire collection was nearly destroyed by a fire in 1925, and it took three years to rebuild, reopening with a new cinema and restaurant. A German bomb destroyed the cinema in 1940, and ironically the figure of Hitler was one of the few figures to survive the attack. Madame Tussaud enjoyed one more piece of immortality – she was the inspiration for Mrs Jarley in Charles Dickens's *The Old Curiosity Shop,* and would no doubt have agreed with Mrs Jarley's sentiment: 'I won't go so far as to say, that, as it is, I've seen wax-work quite like life, but I've certainly seen some life that was exactly like wax-work.'

LONG AGO, BEFORE THE DAYS OF KFC...

In 1172, Londoner William FitzStephen wrote an extended essay on the many delights of London, which included a description of perhaps the first London takeaway. On the river-bank he saw a public cookshop selling 'seasonal foods, dishes roast, fried and boiled, fish of every size, meat for the poor and delicate for the rich, such as venison and various kinds of birds.'

He suggested that it was the perfect solution for when unexpected guests dropped in and there was nothing in the house, that while servants brought the bread, someone could nip down to the river bank and pick up supper. Just the thing – 'since every sort of delicacy is set out for them here'.

A few events that have taken place in London's roundest concert hall

- **1872** Demonstration of Morse apparatus by the Society of Telegraph Engineers and Commissioners
- **1874** Wine Society started with wine left over from an exhibition
- **1881** First ball held, by the Chelsea Hospital for Women
- **1888** First dinner held, for 1400 guests who dined in the amphitheatre and arena, with more in the balconies and boxes
- **1889** Ice Carnival, Bazaar and Festival, including an ice sculpture of the palace of Montreal and snow shoe races
- **1891** Albert Hall registered as a place of worship
- **1895** Salvation Army hold their first rally at the hall
- **1908** First Amateur Boxing Competition
- **1909** Marathon is run indoors: 26 miles and 385 yards was equal to 524 circuits of the arena
- **1910** Chelsea Arts Club Ball, held here every year until 1959
- **1912** Titanic Band Memorial Concert, conducted by Sir Edward Elgar, Henry Wood, Landon Ronald and Thomas Beecham
- **1928** Mass baptism by Elim Evangel of Foursquare gospel group
- **1931** The Ford Motor Show
- **1938** World table tennis championship
- **1941** The first Proms season
- **1943** Secret Government 'pep-talk' on war work for women, with Churchill, Attlee, Eden, Bevin, Cripps and others speaking
- **1951** The Kray twins and Charlie Kray take part in a public boxing match
- **1964** World Open Trampoline Championships
- **1968** Eurovision Song Contest
- **1969** Miss World Contest
- **1970** Tennis first played in the Hall
- **1971** Muhammad Ali boxes
- **1989** Special performance of *Tommy* by The Who
- **1989** Queen's Christmas speech recorded
- **1991** FW de Klerk declares apartheid dead at IOD meeting
- **1991** Sumo wrestling competition
- **1995** *Les Miserables* 10th Anniversary Concert
- **1995** Stephen Hawking lecture
- **1995** David Essex surprised onstage by 'This Is Your Life'
- **1996** Concert for President Nelson Mandela
- **1997** John McEnroe and Bjorn Borg play tennis
- **1998** Andrew Lloyd Webber's 50th birthday celebrations
- **1999** His Holiness the Dalai Lama talks about the New Millennium
- **2002** Sell-out tribute to George Harrison one year after his death

BIG BEN – THE FACTS

- The tower that houses Big Ben is called St Stephen's Tower.
- Big Ben first chimed the hour in July 1859.
- The clock was stopped in 1916, when all public clocks were silenced to prevent them offering directional help to the Germans.
- The chimes of Big Ben were first broadcast on the radio in 1923, and on television in 1949. They are still used in news broadcasts today, and to chime in the New Year.
- In 1944 the clock stopped twice: once when a workmen left a hammer inside and once when a spring broke.
- In 1945 the hammer froze and the clock couldn't strike.
- In 1949 the hands were stopped by swarming starlings.
- The longest stoppage lasted 13 days and took place in 1977 during repairs to the clock.
- The timing of the clock is maintained with old pre-decimalised pennies; adding one to the balance causes the clock to gain two-fifths of a second in 24 hours.

LONDON WORDS

The event of 1775 was the Ranelagh Regatta and Ball, which took place on June 23rd. Early in the afternoon of that day the whole river from London Bridge to Millbank was covered with pleasure boats, and scaffold erections were to be seen on the banks, and even on the top of Westminster Hall. Gambling tables lined the approaches to Westminster Bridge: men went about selling indifferent liquor, Regatta songs and Regatta cards. The river banks now resembled a great fair, and the Thames itself a floating town. Wild calculations fixed the number of the spectators at 200,000, or 'at least' three millions. At 7.30 a cannon signalled the start of the racing-boats, and about 8.30, when the prizes had been awarded, the whole procession began to move 'in a picturesque irregularity towards Ranelagh'. The Directors' barge, with its band playing and gold REGATTA ensign flying, led the way, and the fortunate persons who had ball-tickets landed at Ranelagh Stairs at nine o'clock.

Dancing took place in the Temple of Neptune, a temporary octagon erection in the grounds. Mrs Cornelys had been given seven hundred guineas (it is said) to supply the supper, and it is lamentable to reflect that the supper 'was indifferent, and the wine very scarce'.

Warwick Wroth,
The London Pleasure Gardens in the Eighteenth Century

136 *The number of credit and debit card transactions made per second in London in 2001*

RIOTING IN THE STREETS

In 1381, people held a protest against the hated poll tax which was levied by John of Gaunt on every citizen over the age of 15, including the poorest peasants, to pay for the Hundred Years' War. In what became known as the Peasants' Revolt, ex-soldier Wat Tyler led a band of 10,000 peasants to London, stopping off to attack and plunder anything connected with tax collection. They soon reached London Bridge and poured across the river to attack the north bank, joining forces with other rebels from Essex. John of Gaunt's Savoy Palace was relieved of its treasures and burned to the ground. The mob ran out of control, looting and burning buildings and murdering people in the streets. They were eventually calmed by 14-year-old King Richard II, who offered concessions such as fair rents and the abolition of serfdom. However, the rebels were not yet won over, and the next day they captured the King's Treasurer and Archbishop Sudbury and executed them. But when Wat Tyler was killed the following day, the king turned on the rebels, announced that serfdom would not be abolished, and dared the rebels to defy him. A few did, but were swiftly dispatched by the king's men. The revolt was over.

A FOGGY DAY IN LONDON TOWN

On 5 December 1952, a thick yellow fog descended on London, acrid enough to make the residents' eyes water. Thanks to a warm air front that settled over the Thames valley, the fog hung in the city for four or five days, as the warm air trapped the fog underneath it. Four thousand people died of lung-related problems during the following month, and 12,000 people died overall in a four-month period following the fog, although these figures were denied by the authorities. London had had a history of dense fogs since the start of the industrial revolution, but this one was by far the worst. The fog was so thick that emergency services had to drive around with a policeman walking in front, brandishing a flare. The fog seeped into homes and buildings, and coated everything it touched with a grey film. A performance of *La Traviata* was stopped because the audience could no longer see the stage. At that time, Britain was on the verge of bankruptcy, so the government was exporting the good coal overseas, leaving Britons to burn poorer, smoky coal on their fires. London also had three major power stations in built-up areas, burning coal to produce electricity. The dense fogs continued until the Clean Air Act was finally passed in 1956. It seems ironic that the coal tax, imposed to finance the rebuilding of London after the Great Fire of 1666, was placed on the one substance that made the reconstructed city almost uninhabitable.

Ronnie Scott

While jazz musician Ronnie Scott will be remembered for his legendary jazz club in Soho, he should also be remembered for his self-deprecation and refusal to take life too seriously. In his obituary in the *Daily Telegraph*, Scott was fondly remembered by the writer for his truly terrible jokes, in which he often insulted his audience for being somewhat inert in their response. He would open the evening with some general patter along the lines of 'You should have been here last Tuesday. Somebody should have been here last Tuesday,' with such predictability that customers would occasionally request specific jokes. While he claimed to have opened his club to guarantee that he would have somewhere to play, he was an accomplished musician and played with many of the greats, as well as recording several albums, including one called 'Never Pat a Burning Dog'. His club moved to its current address in Frith Street in 1965, and offered jazz six nights a week, which was radical for Britain at the time. His club played host to the likes of Count Basie and Ella Fitzgerald; The Who held the premiere of *Tommy* there, and Jimi Hendrix gave his last performance there before his untimely death. The club's fortunes declined until it was bought by Chris Blackwell of Island Records, who saved it with a donation of £25,000, given on the understanding that absolutely nothing was to be changed. It was further saved by a jazz revival in the 80s. Scott played sax on the Beatles' 'Lady Madonna'. The title of Ronnie's 1989 biography had the last laugh by immortalising his attitude to his customers: *Let's All Join Hands and Contact the Living*.

HARSH BUT FAIR?

As an example of the severity of custodial sentences in London in the nineteenth century, consider this cautionary tale. At midnight on 19 June 1810, a labourer named Thomas Hart of the parish of Saint Mary Stratford Bow broke into the house of James Lindsay and stole a shirt worth three shillings. He was found guilty – and sentenced to seven years' transportation. However he had reason to be grateful for this lenient sentence. Had it been the sixteenth century, he could have been hanged, which was the penalty for the theft of any goods worth more than a shilling. Instead he spent seven years in Australia – though it is not known if the courts gave him a return ticket for when his sentence was up.

SONGS ABOUT LONDON THAT
WERE NEVER MADE (SADLY)

Acton Baby

Cheam (May Be the Face I Can't Forget)

Do You Know Edgware You're Going To?

East Sheen She Lovely

Esher Really Going Out With Him

Harrow, I Love You (Won't You Tell Me Your Name)

House of the Rising Sunbury

Hatton My Sleeve

Holborn Under A Bad Sign

I Left My Heart in Stamford's Disco

It's Rainham Men

It's Pinner Hard Day's Night

Norbury Told Me (There'd Be Days Like These)

Morden A Feeling

Notting Hill Tear Us Apart

Purple Hayes

Running Up Gants Hill

Sexual Ealing

Sydenham the Dock of the Bay

Thank Kew For The Music

These Boots Were Made For Wapping

Tooting Bec to Happiness

Turnham Japanese

Theydon Bois Are Back In Town

Twenty Four Hours from Tulse Hill

You've Lost That Loving Ealing

THE LION SERMON

The lion sermon is preached on or about 16 October at St Katharine Cree, Leadenhall Street, London EC3, and has been every year since 1649. It was started by Sir John Gayer, once Lord Mayor of London and a big cheese in the East India Company. The sermon is so called because Sir John once found himself face to face with a lion while travelling in Arabia. Defenceless, he took a leaf out of Daniel's book and simply fell to his knees and prayed, whereupon the lion, after sizing him up for a while, turned and slunk off. Overcome with gratitude, Sir John bequeathed a large part of his fortune to charity and endowed a sermon in his home parish, to be delivered on the day of his miraculous reprieve. His story is retold each time, along with a passage from the Book of Daniel.

Width, in metres, of the Crystal Palace built for the Great Exhibition of 1851 139

When he joined the London Zoo volunteer scheme, Alfred hadn't bargained on being assigned to the elephant house

RIOTING IN THE STREETS

The racial tinderbox of Brixton in southwest London erupted into violence after a young black man was stopped and searched there on Saturday 11 April 1981. Hundreds rampaged through the streets, hurling petrol bombs at police, burning cars and looting shops. The rioting began around Railton Road and Atlantic Road, where there had already been clashes between police and black youths the previous night. As the police began to make arrests, more and more rioters joined the fray and the violence increased faster than the police reinforcements could arrive. More than 50 police officers were injured and around 20 people arrested.

The riot was blamed on police action in the preceding weeks, when Operation Swamp sent police out on the streets to stop and question people at random.

The violence was repeated 14 years later in 1995, when the death of 26-year-old Wayne Douglas in police custody sparked riots in the area. A peaceful picket outside the police station turned into an angry march, when police confronted the protestors and it deteriorated. Shots were heard; a policeman was pulled from his motorbike; and officers sealed off a two-mile area around the centre of Brixton to contain the violence. At the post-mortem, Wayne Douglas was found to be suffering from heart disease.

Byron, Lord, *great-uncle of the poet,* shot his friend in a duel: convicted of manslaughter in 1765, fined and released.

Casanova, Giacomo, *seducer, clergyman, soldier, musician, alchemist and librarian.* Imprisoned in 1755 for being a magician (he escaped).

Dadd, Richard: a promising artist who murdered his father in 1843, and spent the rest of his life in a lunatic asylum, creating excessively detailed paintings.

Fraser, Frankie: also known as Mad Frankie for pretending to be mad to avoid being called up. Member of key London gangs, jailed several times. Shot in the head in Clerkenwell in 1991 but survived, describing the incident as 'good fun, good action'.

Ince, George: accused of murder in 1973 but pleaded not guilty, giving as his alibi that he had been in bed with Dolly Kray, wife of the Kray twins' brother Charles. Acquitted.

Knight, Ronnie: notorious London gangster who was arrested for murder. A hitman claimed Knight had hired him for the murder; the hitman was jailed but Knight walked free. Emigrated to Spain, but returned to England in 1994 and jailed for handling money stolen in a robbery committed by his two brothers. Served four years. Later convicted of shoplifting from a north London Waitrose. Fined £200.

Nilsen, Dennis: civil servant who lured men back to his flat in Muswell Hill where he strangled and dismembered them. Discovered when his drains became blocked with human flesh. Confessed to 15 murders and imprisoned for life in 1983.

Payne, Cynthia, brothel-keeper, jailed in 1978 for keeping a disorderly house. Issued vouchers to her customers, which earned her the title Luncheon Voucher Madam. Served six months of her sentence. None of her clients was ever charged.

Queensberry, Marquess of: The man who accused Oscar Wilde of sodomy, Queensberry was himself taken to court for brawling with his own son and once threatened to whip the Foreign Secretary with a dog-whip for being his son's lover.

Rachman, Peter: property owner from Poland who moved to London after World War Two. Developed ways to force out existing tenants by threats and intimidation, which became known as 'Rachmanism'. Many of his buildings became brothels, and he made exorbitant amounts in rent while gambling and consorting with call girls and gangsters. Died in 1962 aged 42.

Sheppard, Jack: eighteenth century burglar who repeatedly escaped from prison. Caught by the thief-taker Jonathan Wild, he refused to hand over his booty in return for his escape. Imprisoned but escaped from Newgate the night before his execution despite leg irons, handcuffs and constant observation. Eventually recaptured and hanged in 1724.

HISTORY IN THE NURSERY

The clock on the church of St Clement Danes plays the tune of the nursery rhyme 'Oranges and Lemons', which is appropriate, as it is the first church mentioned in the rhyme:

> *Oranges and lemons*
> *Say the bells of St Clements;*
> *You owe me five farthings*
> *Say the bells of St Martin's;*
> *When will you pay me?*
> *Say the bells of Old Bailey;*
> *When I grow rich*
> *Say the bells of Shoreditch;*
> *When will that be?*
> *Say the bells of Stepney;*
> *I do not know*
> *Says the great bell of Bow*
> *Here comes a candle to light you to bed*
> *Here comes a chopper to chop off your head*
> *Chop chop chop chop the last man's head!*

The churches mentioned are, in order of appearance:

St Clements, Eastcheap
St Martin Orgar, Cannon Street
St Sepulchre without Newgate
St Leonards, Shoreditch
St Dunstan and All Saints, Stepney
St Mary le Bow, Cheapside

INSPIRED BY A WORM

The first tunnel built under the Thames was designed by Marc Isambard Brunel (1769–1849), the father of Isambard Kingdom Brunel. Brunel Senior fled the French revolution for New York and then London, and at one point found himself in debtor's prison. While incarcerated, he watched a shipworm bore a hole through a piece of wood by passing the munched-up wood pulp through its body and excreting it as it progressed. Once released, Brunel worked on his observation, and eventually constructed a huge drill with corkscrew blades that passed excavated material down its length as it moved forward, which was used to bore a tunnel from Wapping to Rotherhithe. The tunnel took 18 years to build, and 10 men died during its construction. When it opened, it was at first beset by prostitutes and thieves who would lie in wait in the shadows for unsuspecting pedestrians. The East London railway took over the tunnel in 1869, and it now carries the East London Underground line across the river.

*I do not think there is anything deserving the name of
society to be found out of London.*
William Hazlitt, writer

WHO WAS THAT MAN?

Just some of the people suspected of being Jack the Ripper, who
murdered at least five prostitutes in the Whitechapel area in 1888 and
was never caught.

- Joseph Barnett, fish-porter who lived with Mary Jane Kelly, a
  Ripper victim
- WH Bury, hanged for murdering his wife; the marks he left on her
  body were similar to those on one of the Ripper victims
- Prince Albert Victor, Queen Victoria's grandson, supposedly
  driven insane by syphilis
- Alfred Napier Blanchard, who confessed to the murders while
  drinking in a pub and was arrested, but was not believed to be
  telling the truth
- Lewis Carroll, author of *Alice's Adventures in Wonderland*, who,
  according to writer Richard Wallace in his 1996 book, scattered
  clues to his guilt throughout his children's stories
- David Cohen, a Polish Jew, who allegedly hated women and
  especially prostitutes
- Dr T Neill Cream, abortionist and quack doctor, hanged for
  murdering several women
- Frederick Deeming, wife-murderer (twice) and child-killer (four
  times)
- Montague John Druitt, barrister, who committed suicide around
  the time of the murders
- Jill the Ripper, an unknown woman supposedly seen wearing one
  of the victim's clothes
- Severin Klosowski, Polish wife-poisoner
- The Lodger – an occupant of a rented room in Mornington
  Crescent, Camden; the landlord told subsequent lodgers that Jack
  the Ripper had stayed there
- Dr Pedachenko, a Russian spy
- Walter Sickert, the artist, in a complicated conspiracy theory
  involving the royal family
- James Kenneth Stephen, friend of Prince Albert Victor
- Francis Tumblety, quack doctor who hated women and kept a
  collection of wombs in glass jars; the suspect of choice for
  Scotland Yard
- Nicholas Vassily, Russian anarchist and murderer of prostitutes

CAPITAL CONUNDRUMS

Which three men have their statues at the corners of
Trafalgar Square?
Answer on page 153.

LONDON WORDS

It is with great joy that we reproduce here the first and last verses of
Flanders and Swann's musical homage to the big red London bus. The
intermediate verses are equally amusing but, as is often the case with
the bus itself, there was no room for more.

A Transport of Delight
Some talk of a Lagonda,
Some like a smart MG,
Or for Bonnie Army Lorry
They'd lay them doon and dee.
Such means of locomotion
Seem rather dull to us
The driver and conductor
Of a London Omnibus.

...We don't ask much for wages,
We only want fair shares,
So cut down all the stages,
And stick up all the fares.
If tickets cost a pound apiece
Why should you make a fuss?
It's worth it just to ride inside
That thirty-foot-long by ten-foot-wide,
Inside that monarch of the road,
Observer of the Highway Code,
That big six-wheeler
Scarlet-painted
London Transport
Diesel-engined
Ninety-seven horse-power
Omnibus!

Michael Flanders and Donald Swann

QUOTE UNQUOTE

*Sir, the noblest prospect that a Scotchman ever sees, is
the high road that leads him to London.*
Samuel Johnson, writer,
to Boswell, his Scottish biographer

LONDON WORDS

As a journalist for the Sunday Express, *Mrs Cecil Chesterton, OBE, sister-in-law to novelist GK Chesterton, lived on the streets for two weeks to experience life as a homeless woman. Her articles about this experience were published in the* Sunday Express *in 1925 and turned into a book,* In Darkest London, *the following year.*

When she returned to her normal life, Mrs Chesterton set about raising funds to open a women's hostel, and in 1927 the first Cecil House (named after her husband), was opened in Holborn. The Cecil Housing Trust still exists today, to house the homeless and the needy.

The feet of the woman tramp, or street vendor – it is the same thing – are very pitiful to see. They are almost non-human in their shapelessness. Callosities, horny growths, bunions, destroy their contours, running sores are perennial and the efforts of Nature to escape the pain of contact with rough leather, result in distortion of the bone. Ingrowing nails are common; how should it be otherwise? The care of the feet calls for plentiful hot water and requisite toilet accessories; and these women, of whom I write, have not the means to wash their sores. There is, of course, due bathing accommodation in the casual ward of a workhouse, but as I shall show, the thing that survives longest and most fiercely among the destitute, is a passionate fear of restriction, the horror of detention within four walls, under a strange roof. For this reason before they will ask a night's lodging of the Poor Law Guardians they will push endurance to an inhuman limit. This is especially the case with the outcasts of the London streets.

Mrs Cecil Chesterton, *In Darkest London*

SMARTER THAN THE AVERAGE

When a taxi driver in London acquires The Knowledge, a demanding test of their familiarity with London's streets, traffic patterns and key attractions, it actually makes him (or her) smarter. The would-be drivers have to memorise 400 'runs' in the so-called Blue Book, requiring instant recall of around 25,000 different thoroughfares within a six-mile radius of Charing Cross, and a general knowledge of the major roads outside that inner circle. The demands that this places on a driver's spatial skills and memory has been shown to have a beneficial effect. A study carried out at University College in London in 2000 showed that learning and using The Knowledge increases the size of the anterior and posterior hippocampi of the brain, the areas that handle spatial memory and spatial navigation. Compared with control groups and less experienced cab drivers, long-serving taxi drivers had considerably more developed hippocampi. So when London cabdriver Fred Housego won 'Mastermind' in 1980, it should not have come as such a surprise.

Gambling has always been a classless hobby in London, from cockfighting pits to the most exclusive of gentleman's clubs. But it is the latter that saw the greatest gains and losses, as the idle upper classes found a use for their spare time (and spare money).

- In February 1772, **Charles James Fox** lost £11,000 while playing for 24 hours straight at his club, Almack's in Pall Mall. He won back £6,000 two days later, then lost those winnings at Newmarket the same afternoon. He lost a further £10,000 back at Almack's two days later.

- Banker **George Drummond** lost £20,000 in a single game of whist at White's and was forced to resign his position at the family bank.

- **Henry Weston**, 23, resorted to forgery to help clear his gambling debts, and was hanged for the offence in 1796.

- **Lord Robert Spencer**, brother of the Duke of Marlborough, having lost all his money, gambled with a loan and won £100,000, with which he bought an estate in Sussex.

- **Henry Thynne**, also heavily in debt, won back enough in a single night to clear all his debts and buy himself a new house.

- Many gamblers killed themselves after losing everything, including Sir John Bland, Lord Montfort and John Damer, son of Lord Milton.

THE BIG STINK

Until the nineteenth century, London had no waste disposal system. Waste of all kinds was simply emptied into the many waterways, creating a vast open sewer, which was also a source of drinking water for many of the residents (beer was considered a healthier alternative – even for breakfast). Cholera seized the city from 1848–1849, 1853–1854 and 1865–1866, killing around 30,000 people. As the population grew, the situation became unbearable, particularly in the hot summer of 1858. The temperatures shot up to 35°C, creating a smell so bad that the windows of the Houses of Parliament had to be covered with sheets soaked in lime carbide to try to keep out the stench. The authorities tried to disinfect the source with carbolic acid, but to little effect. This was useful to Joseph Bazalgette, the chief engineer of the Metropolitan Board of Works, who in 1855 had begun to draw up plans for a vast sewerage system that comprised 1240 miles of tunnels. The long-suffering government gladly gave permission for construction to begin, and when the work was done, London had some of the cleanest water in Europe. But it took until 1974 before any fish were brave enough to test the new, cleaner waters.

CAPITAL CONUNDRUMS

What's fishy about St John's Wood tube station?
Answer on page 153.

STRANGE EXHIBITS

National Army Museum
The frostbitten fingers of an English soldier who climbed Everest in the 1970s

London Canal Museum
Ice wells 100 feet deep, built in 1860 for the ice cream pioneer, Carlos Gatti

Cuming Museum
The leg of an Egyptian mummy, and a tobacco pouch made from the skin of an albatross from the island of Tristan da Cunha

Horniman
Three voodoo altars and 7,000 musical instruments

Leighton House
Indoor Arab fountain, c.1870

MCC Museum
Stuffed sparrow and the cricket ball that killed it

Royal London Hospital Archives
A fragment of George Washington's false teeth and a video of the remains of the Elephant Man

Sir John Soane Museum
Egyptian sarcophagus, dated c.1370 BC

Bramah Tea and Coffee Museum
World's largest teapot, which is 32 inches high and 78 inches round and makes 800 cups using 3lb of tea

Old Operating Theatre Museum
A bit of nineteenth century brain and the original recipe for Snail Water, which was intended to cure venereal disease

Natural History Museum
A walrus from Hudson Bay, overstuffed by a keen London taxidermist in the 1880s

And the one that got away...
London Transport Museum
used to exhibit the remains of a spiral escalator, but it is sadly now 'almost rubble' and kept in their warehouse at Acton

QUOTE UNQUOTE

She was all for scenery – yes; but she wanted it human and personal, and all she could say was that there would be in London – wouldn't there? – more of that kind than anywhere else.
Henry James, *The Wings of the Dove*

From Park Lane to Wapping, by day and by night,
I've many a year been a roamer,
And find that no lawyer can London indict,
Each street, ev'ry lane's a misnomer.
I find Broad Street, St Giles's, a poor narrow nook,
Battle Bridge is unconscious of slaughter,
Duke's Place cannot muster the ghost of a duke,
And Brook Street is wanting in water.

I went to Cornhill for a bushel of wheat,
And sought it in vain ev'ry shop in,
The Hermitage offered a tranquil retreat
For the jolly Jack hermits of Wapping.
Spring Gardens, all wintry, appear on the wane,
Sun Alley's an absolute blinder,
Mount Street is a level, and Bearbinder Lane
Has neither a bear nor a binder.

No football is kicked up and down in Pall Mall,
Change Alley, alas! never varies,
The Serpentine river's a straitened canal,
Milk Street is denuded of dairies.
Knight's bridge, void of tournaments, lies calm and still,
Butcher Row cannot boast of a cleaver,
And (tho' it abuts on his garden) Hay Hill
Won't give Devon's duke the hay fever.

The Cockpit's the focus of law, not of sport,
Water Lane is affected with dryness,
And, spite of its gorgeous approach, Prince's Court
Is a sorry abode for his Highness.
From Baker Street North all the bakers have fled,
So, in verse not quite equal to Homer,
Methinks I have proved what at starting I said,
That London's one mighty misnomer.

James Smith, *London Misnomers*

BURIED IN BUNHILL FIELDS

A few of the famous names who ended up in Bunhill Fields,
London's non-conformist burial ground
William Blake, poet • John Bunyan, preacher • members of the
Cromwell family • Daniel Defoe, writer • Susanna Wesley, the
mother of John Wesley, founder of Methodism

*The man who is tired of London is tired of
looking for a parking space.*
Paul Theroux, travel writer, who now lives in Hawaii

WONDERWALL

The City Wall was first con-structed by the Romans around AD 200. It took about 10 years to build and ran between two landmarks that were not there when the wall was built, but are now the Tower of London and Blackfriars railway station. It was nearly two miles in length, and enclosed an area of 330 acres. It was between six and nine feet wide and about 18 feet high and incorporated the north and west side of an existing 12-acre Roman fort, and would take about an hour to walk its length. There were large city gates at strategic points along the wall to allow traffic in and out of the City, remnants of which can be seen in the names that remain: Ludgate, Newgate, Aldersgate, Cripplegate, Bish-opsgate and Aldgate.

A series of towers were added in the thirteenth century, and a ditch dug around the outside to improve defences. Two of the 20 towers survive: one at the Barbi-can, and one that has been incor-porated into the Barber-Surgeons Hall. The towers were home to hermits in peacetime. The limits of the city thus remained largely unchanged until the wall was thought no longer necessary for defence in the 1700s, and the ditch had become a nuisance, as it was used as a rubbish dump. Most of the wall was demolished in 1760, and any parts that could not easily be torn down were incorporated into shops. The wall explains that strange name of 'St Botolph's without Aldersgate'; St Botolph's was outside, or without, the city wall. He was the patron saint of trav-ellers, so people would ask for his blessing as they left the city walls. There were originally four St Botolph churches for this pur-pose, although one was destroyed in the Great Fire of London. A few remnants remain within the walls of the Museum of London, and there is another outside Tower Hill tube station.

A DAY AT THE ZOO

Some of London Zoo's more unusual residents
moon jellyfish • superb starling • giant frigate beetle • apple snail
blind cave fish • jackass penguin • bongo • okapi • sand cat
kinkajou • toco toucan • bali starling • aye aye • partula snail
komodo dragon • two-toed sloth • spider monkey
audacious jumping spider

Number of murders carried out in Lambeth, the 'murder capital of **149**
London' in the last 10 years

Around lay the darkened city, a few solid masses, like the Donners-Brebner Building, recognizable on the far side of the twisting strip of water. Then three rapidly moving lights appeared in the southern sky, two more or less side by side, the third following a short way behind, as if lacking acceleration or will power to keep up. They travelled with that curious shuddering jerky movement characteristic of such bodies, a style of locomotion that seemed to suggest the engine was not working properly, might break down at any moment, which indeed it would. This impression that something was badly wrong with the internal machinery was increased by a shower of sparks emitted from the tail. A more exciting possibility was that dragons were flying through the air in a fabulous tale, and climbing into the turret with Curtis had been done in a dream. The raucous buzz could now be plainly heard. In imagination one smelt brimstone. 'They appear to be heading a few degrees to our right, sir,' said Curtis.

The first two cut-out. It was almost simultaneous. The noisy ticking of the third continued briefly, then also stopped abruptly. This interval between cutting-out and exploding always seemed interminable. At last it came; again two almost at once, the third a few seconds later. All three swooped to the ground, their flaming tails pointing upwards, certainly dragons now, darting earthward to consume their prey of maidens chained to rocks.

'Southwark, do you think?'

'Lambeth, sir – having regard to the incurvations of the river.'

'Sweet Thames run softly…'

'I was thinking the same, sir.'

'I'm afraid they've caught it, whichever it was.'

'I'm afraid so, sir.'

The All Clear sounded. We climbed down the iron gangway.

'Do you think that will be all for tonight?'

'I hope so, sir.'

Anthony Powell, *The Military Philosophers*

THE LAST WORD

Sir, if you wish to have a just notion of the magnitude of this city, you must not be satisfied with seeing its great streets and squares, but must survey the innumerable little lanes and courts. It is not in the showy evolutions of buildings, but in the multiplicity of human habitations which are crowded together, that the wonderful immensity of London consists.

Samuel Johnson, writer and diarist

---

150 *Number of workmen who died during the building of the first stone London Bridge in 1549*

DURING THE COMPILATION OF THIS BOOK, THE COMPANION TEAM...

Realised they'd lived in 19 different boroughs between them

Set off on a Monopoly board pub crawl, lost interest very early on, and staggered home at 3am from the Old Kent Road

Criss-crossed the Thames via seven bridges in exactly one hour by car, and 26 minutes by bike

Made a seven-word sentence out of unpronounced letters in the names of London tube stations

Tried to work out why residents of Kensington and Chelsea can park virtually anywhere in London

Mimicked David Blaine's fast, but only lasted until elevenses

Played virtual Mornington Crescent by email, and invented two new rules

Sat for two and a half hours on a stationary train outside Paddington station and then realised it was a Saturday

Actually saw someone going into Centre Point

Unsportingly joined the London Marathon half way through, but still couldn't finish

Overheard someone in an Elephant and Castle pub who actually sounded like Dick van Dyke

Please note that although every effort has been made to ensure accuracy in this book, the above statistics may be the result of less than capital minds.

I don't know what London's coming to – the higher the buildings, the lower the morals.

Noël Coward

The answers. As if you needed them.

P13   Charing Cross, from where all distances are now measured

P26   William Shakespeare

P27   In the south-east corner of Trafalgar Square in a cylindrical structure bearing a huge globe light on top. There is room for one policeman inside

P36   The Circle Line

P49   Samuel Pepys

P53   Waterloo & City: because it names the only two stations that it serves, which are Waterloo and Bank (in the City)

P60   Lord Byron, on the house where he was born in Holles Street

P69   Mansion House and South Ealing

P80   Coventry Street, Glasshouse Street, Piccadilly, Regent Street and Shaftesbury Avenue

P89   It is the name of the largest bell in the clock room of St Paul's Cathedral; Big Ben is the name of the largest bell in St Stephen's Tower in the Palace of Westminster.

P96   It is a corridor in the Royal Courts of Justice. The origin of the nickname is not hard to deduce.

P102   Because eight feet were lost in a storm in 1764.

P108   They are the streets that are most frequently landed on on the Monopoly board.

P115   They are all called George.

P126   Livingstone

P131   Because it was the site of London's first public toilet.

P144   King George IV, Major General Sir Henry Havelock and General Charles James Napier

P147   It's the only tube station not to contain any of the letters of the word 'mackerel'.

FURTHER READING

The Absolutely Essential Guide to London,
David Benedictus

Capital Disasters, John Withington

The Very Best of the Daily Telegraph Books of Obituaries,
edited by Hugh Massingberd

Do Not Pass Go, Tim Moore

Eccentric London, Benedict le Vay

Footprint Guide to London, Charlie Godfrey-Faussett

A Literary Guide to London, Ed Glinert

Location London, Mark Adams

The London Compendium, Ed Glinert

Mysterious Britain, Janet and Colin Bord

The Nicholson London Pub Guide

Old Customs and Ceremonies of London,
Margaret Brentnall

Permanent Londoners, Judi Culbertson and Tom Ran

Subterranean City, Antony Clayton

Secret London, Andrew Duncan

The Penguin Dictionary of British Place Names,
Adrian Room

Top 10 of Everything 2004, Russell Ash

What's In A Name, Cyril M Harris

Walking Notorious London, Andrew Duncan

Encyclopedia of London Crime and Vice, Fergus Linnane

The London Nobody Knows, Geoffrey Fletcher

London's Disused Underground Stations, JE Connor

ACKNOWLEDGEMENTS

We gratefully acknowledge permission to reprint extracts of copyright material in this book from the following authors, publishers and executors:

Extract from *Candida* by George Bernard Shaw reproduced by permission of the Society of Authors on behalf of the Bernard Shaw Estate

Monody on the Death of Aldersgate Station by John Betjeman, reproduced by permission of John Murray Publishers

The Man Who Was Thursday by GK Chesteron reproduced by permission of AP Watt Ltd on behalf of The Royal Literary Fund.

Extract from *The Little Princesses* by Marion Crawford reproduced by permission of The Orion Publishing Group

Extract from *Soho in the Fifties* by Daniel Farson, reproduced by permission of AM Heath Ltd

'*A Transport of Delight*' reproduced by permission of the Estates of Michael Flanders and Donald Swann 2004

Extract from *A Room with a View* by E M Forster reproduced by permission of The Provost and Scholars of King's College, Cambridge and the Society of Authors as the Literary Representatives of the Estate of EM Forster

HM Howgrave-Graham, *Light and Shade at Scotland Yard*

Extract from *Kim* by Rudyard Kipling, reproduced by permission of A P Watt Ltd on behalf of the National Trust for Places of Historical Interest or Natural Beauty.

Extract from *In Search of England* by H V Morton, published by Methuen Publishing Ltd, copyright © Marion Wasdell and Brian de Villiers

Extract from *The Military Philosophers* by Anthony Powell, reproduced by permission of David Higham Associates

Extract from *Scoop* by Evelyn Waugh (copyright © Beneficiaries of the Evelyn Waugh Settlement 1938) by permission of PFD on behalf of the Beneficiaries of the Evelyn Waugh Settlement

Scoop by Evelyn Waugh reproduced by permission of the publishers LIttle,Brown and Company.

INDEX

Abbeys, cathedrals and churches 25, 31, 33, 48, 63, 68, 85, 123

Actors 29, 123,

Animals 10, 23, 49, 72, 73, 100, 102, 105, 107, 149

Archaeology 10

Architecture 35, 44, 46, 50, 51, 53, 73, 84, 90, 97, 99

Art and artists 20, 40, 43, 52, 82, 89, 109, 118

Art galleries and museums 11, 17, 40, 45, 147

Aubrey, John 84

Auctions 20, 41, 88

Bankhead, Tallulah 117

Berger, John 21

Bernard Shaw, George 20, 114

Betjemen, Sir John 91

Bierce, Ambrose 39

Blaine, David 63

Blume, Mary 99

Body snatchers 82, 86

Bridges 10, 17, 38, 53, 61, 67, 92

British Library 74, 118

Cabs and cabbies 28, 113, 126, 145

Capital conundrums 13, 25, 27, 36, 49, 52, 60, 69, 80, 89, 96, 102, 108, 115, 126, 131, 144, 147

Carter, Angela 11

Casson, Sir Hugh 92

Caxton, William 95

Ceremonies and traditions 16, 72, 76, 100, 113, 139

Chesterton, Mrs C 145

Chesterton, GK 70

Clocks 10, 105, 136

Cockneys 21, 50

Colman, George 120

Conan Doyle, Sir Arthur 87

Crawford, Marion 26

Curiosities 17, 18, 19, 29, 43, 44, 57, 63, 105, 109, 110

Demonstrations and riots 13, 21, 33, 41, 47, 57, 81, 96, 137, 140

de Quincey, Thomas 133

Dickens, Charles 11, 73, 115

Disasters 25, 45, 64, 90, 109, 112, 124, 146

Disraeli, Benjamin 58, 85

Demises 17, 25, 45, 46, 51, 58, 64, 73, 82, 84, 86, 109, 112, 123, 124, 137, 148

Dunbar, William 32

Emerson, Ralph Waldo, 51, 74

Executions 65, 89, 119, 123, 138

Facts and figures 16, 106, 118, 122, 133

Famous Londoners 24, 29, 34, 39, 108, 115, 123, 148

Famous visitors 12, 14, 24, 39, 63, 88, 134

Farson, Daniel 112

Festivals 76, 114

Films and locations 46, 75, 101, 126, 132

Fires 42, 52, 64, 68, 120, 127

Flanders, Michael 144

Flaubert, Gustav 91

Forster, EM 131

Frost fairs 67

Games 30, 110, 146

Georgian London 13, 19, 23, 38

Ghosts 15, 111

Gibbs, Philip 96

Global influences 33, 62

Gorbachev, Mikhail 131

Graffiti 74

Hare, Augustus 17

Hazlitt, William 143

Hicks, Seymour 23

Historic London 33, 42, 48, 114

Hone, William 87

Howgrave-Graham, HM 60

Hurd, Douglas 122

Inventions and discoveries 30, 34, 94, 125, 131

James, Henry 12

Johnson, Samuel 144, 150

King George VI 57
Kipling, Rudyard 78
Kronenberger, Louis 102
Lamb, Charles 66
le Carré, John 106
Lenin, Vladimir Ilyich 93
Literary London 37, 39, 50, 44, 59, 74, 77, 123
London buses 13, 144
London, Jack 125
London Underground 26, 28, 54, 55, 66, 69, 71, 83, 102, 103, 109, 121, 124
Lord Balfour of Burleigh 31
Lost property 86
Marathons 72, 79
Markets 63, 81, 107, 111, 127
Mayhew, Henry 42
Melville, Herman 27
Middle ages, the 21, 49, 52, 85, 128
Midler, Bette 47
Monsarrat, Nicholas 34
Morton, HV 45
Murders 17, 73, 85, 89, 108, 141, 143
Music and musicians 18, 20, 58, 74, 80, 123, 138, 139
Norman London 32, 53, 134
Oddities 46, 61, 113, 119, 147
Origins 22, 60, 85, 101
Osborne, John 128
Patron Saints 40
Pearly Kings and Queens 18
Pepys, Samuel 56, 104
Phobias 47
Politics and parliament 47, 52, 127
Powell, Anthony 150
Prehistoric London 10, 48, 56, 102
Printing and publishing 41, 70, 95
Pritchett, VS 62
Pubs 18, 34, 39, 65, 89, 104, 108, 111
Railways 17, 66, 142
Roman London 32, 42, 48, 68, 114, 149
Royal palaces 10, 31, 32, 51, 52, 65, 68
Royal peccadilloes 26, 52, 77, 120, 122
Royal traditions 16, 33, 40, 72
Royalty 44, 57, 84, 97, 127
Sampson, Anthony 75
Sex 24, 32, 49, 92, 93, 141
Seventeenth century 18, 21, 25, 26, 45, 64, 73, 99, 107, 127
Smith, James 148
Sports 16, 27, 67, 72, 79, 87, 116, 130
Statues and monuments, 13, 56, 62, 99
Street lore 22, 73, 100, 119
Streets 58, 109, 113
Subterranean relics 82, 90
Subterranean city 84, 85, 97, 130
Swann, Donald 144
Taxes 21, 52, 137
Thackeray, William 129
Thames, the 10, 27, 31, 67, 72, 84, 92, 102, 105, 142
Theatres and concert halls 25, 29, 79, 127, 128, 135
Theroux, Paul 149
Tourist attractions 10, 11, 13, 31, 32, 81, 136
Tower of London, the 65
Twain, Mark 37
Victorian London 14, 18, 25, 27, 28, 31, 71, 80, 146
Villains and rogues 10, 23, 26, 44, 51, 65, 97, 104, 108, 117, 138, 141, 143, 146
Walpole, Horace 70
War 38, 42, 46, 56, 84, 92, 96, 109
Waugh, Evelyn 98
Wilde, Oscar 24, 81, 107
Woolf, Leonard 73
Wordsworth, William 51, 66
Wroth, Warwick 136
Yeats, WB 37
Zoo 73, 129, 149

FILL YOUR BOOKSHELF AND YOUR MIND

The Birdwatcher's Companion Twitchers, birders, ornithologists and garden-tickers: there are many species of birdwatcher, and you're all catered for by this unique book. ISBN 1-86105-833-0

The Cook's Companion Whether your taste is for foie gras or fry-ups, this tasty compilation is an essential ingredient in any kitchen, boiling over with foodie fact and fiction. ISBN 1-86105-772-5

The Gardener's Companion For anyone who has ever put on a pair of gloves, picked up a spade and gone out into the garden in search of flowers, beauty and inspiration. ISBN 1-86105-771-7

The Golfer's Companion Bogeys and shanking, plus fours and six irons, the alleged etiquette of caddies – all you need to know about the heaven and hell of golf is in this unique book. ISBN 1-86105-834-9

The Ideas Companion This fascinating book tells the stories behind the trademarks, inventions, and brands that we come across every day. ISBN 1-86105-835-7

The Legal Companion From lawmakers to lawbreakers, this fascinating compilation offers a view of the oddities, quirks, origins and stories behind the legal world. ISBN 1-86105-838-1

The Literary Companion Whether your Dickens is Charles or Monica, your Stein Gertrude or Franken, here's your book. Literary fact and fiction from Rebecca East to Vita Sackville-West. ISBN 1-86105-798-9

The London Companion From Edgware to Morden, Upminster to Ealing, here's your chance to explore the history and mystery of the most exciting capital city in the world. ISBN 1-86105-799-7

The Moviegoer's Companion Explore the strange and wonderful world of movies, actors, cinemas and salty popcorn in all their glamorous glory from film noir to Matt LeBlanc. ISBN 1-86105-797-0

The Politics Companion The history, myths, great leaders and greater liars of international politics are all gathered around the hustings in this remarkable compilation. ISBN 1-86105-796-2

The Sailing Companion This is the book for everyone who knows their starboard from their stinkpot, and their Raggie from their stern – and anybody who wants to find out. ISBN 1-86105-839-X

The Traveller's Companion For anyone who's ever stared at a distant plane, wondered where it's going, and spent the rest of the day dreaming of faraway lands. ISBN 1-86105-773-3

The Walker's Companion If you've ever laced a sturdy boot, packed a cheese sandwich, and stepped out in search of stimulation and contemplation, then this book is for you. ISBN 1-86105-825-X

The Wildlife Companion Animal amazements, ornithological oddities and botanical beauties abound in this compilation of natural need-to-knows and nonsense for wildlife-lovers. ISBN 1-86105-770-9